Herman Heuser

Chapters of Bible study

A popular introduction to the study of the Sacred Scriptures

Herman Heuser

Chapters of Bible study
A popular introduction to the study of the Sacred Scriptures

ISBN/EAN: 9783744726948

Printed in Europe, USA, Canada, Australia, Japan

Cover: Foto ©Lupo / pixelio.de

More available books at **www.hansebooks.com**

CHAPTERS OF BIBLE STUDY

OR

A POPULAR INTRODUCTION TO THE STUDY OF THE SACRED SCRIPTURES

BY

THE REV. HERMAN J. HEUSER

PROF. OF SCRIPTURAL INTRODUCTION AND EXEGESIS, ST. CHARLES SEMINARY, OVERBROOK, PA.

The Cathedral Library Association
123 E. 50th Street
New York
1895

Nihil Obstat:
> D. J. McMAHON,
>> *Censor Librorum.*

Imprimatur:
> ✠ MICHAEL AUGUSTINE,
>> *Archbishop of New York.*

LOAN STACK

COPYRIGHT BY JOSEPH H. McMAHON, 1895.

PREFACE.

The following pages are printed from notes used in a series of lectures before the "Catholic Summer School of America" at Plattsburgh. They are neither an exhaustive nor a scientific exposition, but are meant as a suggestive introduction, in popular form, to the intelligent reading of the Bible. Some of the answers to questions proposed by members of the "School" during the course have been inserted where it seemed most suitable.

I take occasion here to express my deep appreciation of the courtesy shown to its visitors by the Directors of the "Catholic Summer School." Their self-sacrificing spirit has secured to the organization the earnest co-operation of many gifted men and women animated by that refined Catholic feeling which constitutes the highest type of a truly cultured society. Nothing could have placed the institution on a firmer basis, or could better have given it that guarantee of success to which the last session has borne witness.

H. J. H.

CONTENTS.

		PAGE
I.	The Ancient Scroll,	7
II.	Strange Witnesses,	19
III.	The Testimony of a Confession,	25
IV.	The Stones Cry Out,	27
V.	Heavenly Wisdom,	31
VI.	The Vicious Circle,	40
VII.	The Sacred Pen,	41
VIII.	The Melody and Harmony of the "Vox Cœlestis,"	48
IX.	The Voice from the Rock,	50
X.	A Source of Culture,	52
XI.	The Creation of New Letters,	63
XII.	English Style,	66
XIII.	Friends of God,	69
XIV.	The Art of Prospecting,	72
XV.	Using the Kodak,	75
XVI.	The Interpretation of the Image,	82

		PAGE
XVII.	"Deus Illuminatio Mea,"	89
XVIII.	Rush-Lights,	92
XIX.	The Use and the Abuse of the Bible,	96
XX.	The Vulgate and the "Revised Version,"	115
XXI.	The Position of the Church,	132
XXII.	Mysterious Characters,	140
XXIII.	Conclusion,	147
XXIV.	Appendix,	151

CHAPTERS OF BIBLE STUDY.

I.

THE ANCIENT SCROLL.

If a mysteriously-written document were brought to you, and its bearer assured you that it contained a secret putting you in possession of a great inheritance by establishing your relationship to an ancient race of kings, of which you had no previous knowledge, how would you regard such a document?

You would examine its age, the character of the manuscript, the quality of the paper or parchment; you would ask how it had come to you, and by whom it had been transmitted through successive generations before it reached you. And when, after careful inquiry, you had established the age and authenticity of the document, then you would study its contents, examine the nature of its provisions, and, having clearly understood its meaning, ask yourself: How can I carry out the conditions laid down in this testament, in order that I may obtain the full benefit of the generous bequest left by my noble ancestor?

It is on similar lines that I propose to treat our subject. We shall take up the Bible just as we would take up any other written work, requiring, for the time being, simply so much faith—no more, but also no less than we would exact in the fair examination of any other work, whether of fact or of fiction.

When we have assured ourselves that the Bible is really as old and as truthful a record of history as it pretends to be, and that it has for it such human testimony as leads us to admit historic facts in general, we shall occupy ourselves with its contents, with the influence which this wonderful book, this ancient testament of our royal Sire, exercises upon the heart, the mind, the general culture, by which it leads us to our inheritance, and enables us to assume our place in our destined home.

The Bible, looking upon it as a merely human production, is a collection of documents of various antiquity, containing historic records of successive generations, going back to a very remote period. It relates the valiant deeds of valiant men and women, written either by themselves or by men of their own race. It contains, furthermore, a great number of principles, doctrines, rules, and laws for the moral and external government of individuals and communities, particularly of the families and tribes of the Hebrew nation. Finally, we find in this ancient scroll certain predictions and prophecies which, if we can show that they were definitely made long in advance of the events foretold by them, become a strong argument in favor of the supernatural origin of the work. However, this last point we shall leave entirely out of view for the present.

It is very clear that the book which we have in our hands, and which we call the Bible, or The Book *par excellence*, has been printed and reprinted during four hundred years, in millions of copies, all of which agree substantially, not excepting the Bible of the so-called "reformers," with whom, on the whole, we differ rather in the interpretation than in the wording of its contents. There are indeed some disagreements on subjects touching religious doctrines, which, whilst very important if we accept the Sacred Scriptures as the inspired word of God, hardly count for anything in a merely historical work; and this is the light in which we regard the Bible just at present.

The Bibles which are printed to-day are practically and substantially the same as those which were printed four hundred years ago. A great number of copies of first editions in different languages may still be found in public and private libraries. The New Testament version, from which Luther principally made his translation, was an edition by the well-known humanist, Erasmus. All the modern European translations, including that made into English five hundred years ago by Wiclif, had for their original an ancient Latin version which was employed in the service of the churches, and of which copies in manuscript, made over a thousand years ago, are still extant. One of the oldest uncial Latin manuscripts is the "Vercelli Gospels," attributed to the hand of Eusebius. The Corpus Christi College Library at Cambridge has a manuscript copy said to have been made by St. Augustine. Of Greek copies we have a very famous one in the Vatican Library, probably the oldest preserved in the world—about 350; another manuscript, called the Codex Sinaiticus, is in the Imperial Library of St. Petersburg; and a third, of nearly the same age (IV. century), is the "Codex Alexandrinus," at present in the British Museum. Manuscripts older than these are wanting, not only of the Bible, but of any other book, except fragments of writings on parchment and certain manuscripts rescued from Egyptian tombs, and papers discovered in the recent excavations of Herculaneum, near Naples, in Italy. Parchment, on account of the expensive preparation required to make it suitable material for writing, was sparingly used by the ancients at any time. They preferred to employ the so-called papyrus, made of the fibrous pith of a kind of rush growing abundantly in Egypt, and brought to Europe by Eastern merchants. This, and other kinds of vegetable fibre from which paper suitable for writing was prepared since the days when Moses, as we must presume, practised the art of writing in the schools of Egypt, do not withstand the destructive influence of time. Experience proves that the ordinary atmosphere has completely corroded cotton paper of nine hundred years ago; the same is true of the linen paper made in the time of Albertus Magnus and St. Thomas. Those exceptional treasures of Egyptian papyrus referred to above, which have been found of late years, owe their preservation to the fact that they were enclosed in almost air-tight tombs, in a singularly dry climate; the same is the case with regard to the manuscripts discovered in Herculaneum, which have been kept hermetically sealed by the tight lava-cover from Mount Vesuvius for a space of more than seventeen hundred years.

However, among such manuscripts as have been preserved under ordinary conditions, by far the greatest number are copies, in various tongues, of the Bible, and some of these carry us back to the fourth century. We have Bible manuscripts written on paper in Hebrew, Syriac, Greek, Latin, in the dialects of the Copts, the Arabs, the Armenians, the Persians, the Ethiopians, the Slavs, and the Goths, who were among the earliest nations converted to Christianity. Now all these manuscript Bibles, more than fourteen centuries old, substantially correspond to our Catholic Bibles of this day.

The early Christian missionaries who introduced the word of God to the pagan nations speaking a strange tongue must have had some uniform source whence to make their translations. So many persons in different parts of the world, unacquainted with one another's language, could not, except by some incredible miracle, have composed out of their fancy so large a book, agreeing page for page, nay, line for line. They must have had some original at their disposal whence to make a uniform copy. The fact is, we find that original book in the churches of Italy, Greece, Asia, and Africa. The apostolic Fathers speak of it as known to everybody; they read from it on Sundays and festivals; they quote long passages, and the young candidates for Holy Orders are taught, like the Hebrew levites of old, to memorize the psalms and moral books of the Bible. Among these witnesses is St. Clement of Rome. According to Tertullian, who lived near his time, he was ordained by St. Peter the Apostle; at any rate, St. Paul speaks of him in his Epistle to the Philippians. Other disciples of the Apostles were St. Ignatius, Bishop of Antioch, St. Polycarp, the friend of St. John. These are followed by St. Justin, who wrote a famous defence of the Catholic faith called the " Apology," which he presented to the Emperor Antoninus. The latter, convinced of the young convert's sincerity, put a stop to the cruel persecutions which were then going on against the Christians. The Emperor Marcus Aurelius also received a copy of the "Apology" from St. Justin. In this well-known work the Saint states that "*the Gospels, together with the writings of the prophets, are publicly read in the assemblies of the Christians.*" [1] He also affirms that they were written in part by the Apostles themselves and partly by their disciples. This was shortly after the year 138, when men were still alive who had conversed with St. Paul, and who could well remember the sweet admonitions of brotherly love given

[1] *Apolog.*, I. 67.

The Ancient Scroll. 13

by the aged St. John, who tells us that he had seen with his own eyes the things which he writes.[1] The chain of apostolic writers from St. Peter to St. Augustine, *i. e.*, from the first century to the fourth or fifth, bears witness that this wonderful book was used in every Christian community from the regions of the Jordan, whence St. Justin came, to the confines of Spain, where Isidore of Cordova wrote his commentaries; from the northernmost part of Dalmatia, where Titus had preached the doctrine delivered him by St. Paul, to the limit of the African desert, whence one of the oldest Latin versions of the Scriptures was brought to St. Ambrose.

It is interesting to be able to cite the testimony of pagan as well as of Jewish writers concerning the great events which the Christian Gospels record. We have the historic fact of Christ's person and work attested in the "Annals" of Tacitus, the greatest of Roman historians,[2] who was consul of Rome in 97. His statements are corroborated by Suetonius, secretary to the Emperor Adrian, by Pliny, the Viceroy of Bithynia and friend of the Emperor Trajan, by the Jewish writers Philo of Alexandria, a contemporary of Christ, and the historian Flavius Josephus, and by the rabbis who collated the traditions of the Talmud. All these, whilst they wrote but briefly of the subject, bear indirect witness to the belief and to the practice by the earliest

[1] Ep. St. John, chap. i. 1.   [2] Tacit., *Annal.*, xv. 38–44.

Christians of the Gospel precepts, although the books of the New Testament had not at that time been formed into a definite canon. Thus the unbroken evidence of the existence of the Christian Scriptures goes back to the very time of their first composition.

We come to the Old Testament. That the Jews in the time of Christ possessed a collection of sacred books is recorded on every page of the New Testament, of whose authentic source there can be no reasonable doubt. There are altogether about two hundred and seventy passages in the New Testament books which are quotations from the Old Testament. There are innumerable references in the Gospels and Epistles, and in the early Christian writers, to the sacred law of the Jews, among whom the first converts were made; for these converts continued to use the Mosaic writings and the prophetical books. Christ Himself had beautifully illustrated this practice, from the first, in His teaching. "He came to Nazareth," St. Luke tells us, "where He was brought up; and He went into the synagogue, according to His custom, on the sabbath day; and He rose up to read. And the Book of Isaias the Prophet was delivered unto Him. And as He unfolded the book He found the place where it was written: *The spirit of the Lord is upon me, wherefore He hath anointed me; to preach the gospel to the poor He hath sent me; to heal the contrite of heart. To preach deliverance to the captives, and sight to the blind; to set at liberty them that are bruised; to preach the acceptable year of the Lord, and the day of reward.* And when He had folded the book He restored it to the minister and sat down. And the eyes of all in the synagogue were fixed on Him. And He began to say to them: *This day is fulfilled this Scripture in your ears.* And all gave testimony to Him." [1]

Any attempt to corrupt the Old Testament writings, or to change and destroy them, even in part, became impossible after the Gospels had been written. It would at once have aroused marked attention among both Jews and Christians, who with equal reverence regarded the Book as the sacred and inviolable word of God, however mutually hostile their feelings were regarding the interpretation of its meaning. For if ever there existed a document whose authority was sanctioned and whose preservation was guaranteed by the severest laws and most minute precautions, it was the code of sacred writings known to the Jews as the " Law and the Prophets." It was read in every synagogue on the sabbath and festival days. Every Jew above the age of twelve was obliged to repeat certain parts of the Sacred Book each day, morning and night. Thrice dispersed among the Gentile nations, north, west, and south, the Jews carried with them the book of the Law and the Prophets, and we find them repeat its sweet words of hope and trust in Jehovah by the rivers of Babylon as under

[1] St. Luke iv. 16–22.

the glimmer of the torchlights in the caverns of Samaria or rocky Arabia. Their faces were forever turning towards Jerusalem. Nay, when the language of their fathers had ceased to be spoken during generations of enforced exile, the children still repeated the Hebrew words of the Law in the temple, even though they had versions made for the people by rabbis who were under sacred vow not to change an iota of the Lord's written word. We have in the present Hebrew Bibles some remnant of the traditional care with which the Jew guarded the letter of the Law, whatever might be the spirit in which he interpreted it. In order that the Sacred Text might never be tampered with, even by the addition or omission of a single letter or word, the scribes were obliged to count the verses, words, and characters of each book. They knew by heart every peculiarity of grammatical or phonetic expression. Thus the young rabbi must verify that the Book of Genesis contains 1,534 verses; that the exact middle of the book, counting every letter from the beginning and from the end, occurs in chapter xxvii. 40. He knew that there were ten verses in the Scriptures beginning and ending with the letter נ (*nun*) (as in Lev. xiii. 9); two in which every word ends with the letter ם (*mem*). The letter ע (*ayin*), in Ps. lxxx. 14, is the exact middle of the Psalter. The letter א (*aleph*) occurs 42,377 times, ב (*beth*) 38,218 times, ג (*ghimel*) 29,537 times, and so of every letter in the alphabet. These, and a thousand other

The Ancient Scroll. 17

peculiarities which made the corruption of the Hebrew text an almost absolute impossibility, were in later ages collected into a glossary called the Masorah, which forms a sort of separate commentary to the Bible. If you open the Hebrew volume of the Old Testament, just as it is printed to-day, you will find many of these warnings inserted in the very text. Thus at the end of the Book of Chronicles we have this sentence: "The printer is not at fault, for the sum total of verses in the whole Book of Chronicles is 1656." Then, lest the reader might forget this number, a verse is attached which contains the letters representing the same number. The verse, which is taken from the I. Samuel vi. 13, reads: "*They saw the ark and rejoiced in seeing it.*" Just as the words "*MeDiCaL VIrtue*" might stand in English for the same number.

Many other peculiarities in the manner of copying the Hebrew text have been transmitted for ages without change. Thus in the Book of Numbers xi. 1 we find the letter נ (*nun*) written backward ן, to express more emphatically the meaning of "perversity," mentioned in the verse. In Job xxxviii. 13 the letter ע (*ayin*) in the word רְשָׁעִים (*reshachim*), "ungodly," is raised above the line, to indicate how God will shake up into the air, like chaff, the ungodly of whom the Prophet speaks.

But it is needless to point out in detail all the odd

precautions which were invented by the rabbis that they might exercise a most rigorous control over the Hebrew text; and although these methods are the results of a later school of Hebraists, they go to show the sense of responsibility which the Jews must always have felt regarding the preservation of the ancient Testament. Even at this day you can hardly discover a substantial departure from the original in the numerous manuscript copies extant. Kennicott, an English Biblical scholar, brought together five hundred and eighty Hebrew manuscripts of the Bible which, after careful study and comparison, revealed scarcely any differences of the text. An Italian, Prof. de Rossi, who died in 1831, had collected seven hundred and ten manuscripts, and had seen in various libraries one hundred and thirty-four more, all of which he examined critically without finding any notable differences. I am speaking, remember, of such differences as would affect the historical identity of these manuscript copies with their original. It would be folly to assert that these manuscripts, which reached the number of over 1,600, are copies made by the same scribes; for some of them were discovered in Arabia, others in old Jewish settlements in China; one, the oldest in existence, as some believe, was found in a synagogue in the Crimea, by a Jewish rabbi named Abraham Firkeowicz.

II.

STRANGE WITNESSES.

If there remained no trace of the original writings of the Old Testament books preserved for us in the Hebrew tongue, we should still possess very reliable witnesses of ancient date to testify to their existence in substantially the same form in which we have them; for the children of Jewish exiles, who were forced gradually to substitute the language of their conquerors for their mother tongue, had well authenticated translations for their use in the synagogues. The most remarkable of such translations is the so-called Greek Septuagint, commonly believed to have been made for the Alexandrian Library by seventy Jewish rabbis at the request of King Ptolemy Philadelphus. We shall have occasion, later on, to revert to the significance of this Greek version. For the present it is only necessary to mention that it was so highly esteemed by the Jews themselves that they used it for several centuries in their reading to the people, many of whom understood only the Greek.

Even the enemies of the Jews bear witness to the unchanged character of the oldest portion of the Hebrew Bible for centuries before the coming of our Lord.

About the year 536 B. C., on the return of the Jewish exiles from Babylon, the Samaritans, a mixed race of Jewish and Aramaic stock, sought from the temple authorities at Jerusalem the privilege of worshipping with the rest of the Jews in the holy city. This was refused. Shortly afterwards one of the priests at Jerusalem was excommunicated for having married the daughter of a Samaritan prince. He sought refuge in Samaria, and having built a temple on Mount Garizim, induced the people to worship according to the Mosaic Law. They were found to possess a copy of the Pentateuch, which they had transcribed in Samaritan characters; and whilst the Jews of Southern Palestine held no communication with them, and the Samaritans on their part looked upon the Jews as schismatics who had changed the ancient observances of the Law, yet both recognized the same sacred code as the rule of their conduct and religion.

A copy of this valuable version, which at a later date was translated into the actual Samaritan dialect, was discovered at Damascus in 1616, and has since been printed in several editions at Paris and London. It is of great importance, as it establishes a perfect accord with the reading of the Jewish Hebrew text. These versions, made at different times, in places widely apart, and by men who were decidedly hostile to each other on religious as well as on national grounds, force us to admit a well-fixed, universally known, and trusted original of the books of Moses; for where there is a copy there must be something copied from, just as when we see the well-defined shadow of an object we know that the object itself exists.

The antiquity of the Hebrew Bible is indeed attested by many no less conclusive arguments than those we have given, which, from the historian's point of view, stamp it as the most important monument of antiquity which we have, and whose genuine character is proved by the most trustworthy documentary evidence. There is no page of historical account in existence to-day that has such overwhelming testimony in favor of its authentic origin as these books of the Bible. Known by generations as the inviolable law of God, guarded with scrupulous solicitude as their greatest religious treasure, read sabbath after sabbath in the synagogues, not alone of Palestine, but of Arabia, Assyria, Egypt, Asia Minor, Greece, and Rome—in short, wherever the sons of Abraham had been dispersed in the course of more than twenty centuries—who was it, friend or foe, that could have dared to change this royal mandate of the Most High to His chosen people! If a man were to-day to print a copy of the Constitution, or a history of the formation of the American Republic, introducing some hitherto unheard-of statements, or omitting some important words or facts, how long would such imposition remain unnoticed or unchallenged? Yet it would be infinitely easier in our times, and under our conditions, for such change to pass unnoticed than it would have been among the Jews. The Oriental races are intensely averse to anything that threatens to alter their traditions. The customs of the Eastern peoples to-day are the same as they are described by Isaias seven hundred years before Christ, and the Jew of Isaiah's time reflects in every act the manners of another seven hundred years before, when Moses describes his people as imitating the domestic virtues and habits of Abraham's day, a time which carries us back still another seven centuries. A thousand years make no perceptible change in Oriental civilization. You may see it every day. Take as a ready instance Algeria, visited annually by many Americans, who go to Europe by the southern route. It is a coast city, lying in the full glare of European civilization; nay, modern life has forced itself upon this town with the captivating aggressiveness of French manners, French magnificence, French soldiery, and a system of commerce which, within the last sixty years, has caused the European population to outnumber the original Arab inhabitants of Algiers by two-thirds. Yet the daily and forced contact, for two whole generations, between the Arab and the European has produced hardly any change in the habits of the former. The Mussulman passes through the splendid streets of the French portion of the town when necessity urges him, in silence and with apparent disdain. He prefers his cavern-like habitation, with small square holes for windows, and an iron grating instead of glass, to the spacious and lightsome palaces built by the French and English colonists. The Arab woman feels no desire for the pretty vanities of modern fashion, for the graceful freedom and intellectual intercourse with men; she conceals her form in the traditional wide robe of the East, with a veil over her head, a row of shining coins or beads hanging down from the forehead, and a kerchief over her face hiding all but the gazelle-like eyes. You see in that one city, open to the constant changes arising from the innumerable relations of travel and commerce, two worlds of men: one busy, fitful, gay, and splendidly modern; the other silent, immovable, almost scornful, and in dwelling and dress, in manner and language, just the same as you might have observed them ages ago.

Such precisely were the people who guarded and delivered to us the books of the Old Testament. Their religious, civil, and domestic practices, everywhere and at all times of their history, correspond so perfectly with what we read in any part of this volume that, even if portions of the Bible were lost, we should have the living tradition to witness to the omission, since we know that the life of the Hebrew was ever subject to the regulations of the law of Jehovah, which was to him the supreme expression of all that is great and good and wise.

"Uniformity of belief and ritual practice," says the Protestant Geikie,[1] " was the one grand design of the

[1] "Life of Christ," chap. xvii.

founders of Judaism; the moulding the whole religious life of the nation to such a machine-like discipline as would make any variation from the customs of the past well-nigh impossible. A universal, death-like conservatism, permitting no change in successive ages, was established as the grand security for a separate national existence. ... For this end, not only was that part of the Law which concerned the common life of the people —their sabbaths, feast-days, jubilees, offerings, sacrifices, tithes, the Temple and Synagogue worship, civil and criminal law, marriage, and the like—explained, commented on, and minutely ordered by the Rabbis, but also that portion of it which related only to the private duties of individuals in their daily religious life." And to this day the orthodox Jew observes the same rites and ceremonies which marked the service of his forefathers, whether in Judea or Samaria, on the banks of the Nile under the Ptolemies, at Babylon under the Seleucides, or at Niniveh under Nabuchodonoser. "What event of profane history," writes the Abbé Gainet, "can boast of an unbroken succession of 3,500 anniversaries such as those of which we have assurance in the history of the Jews?"[1]

---

[1] La Bible sans la Bible, vol. I., Etude préliminaire.

III.

THE TESTIMONY OF A CONFESSION.

The argument of the last chapter leads us to another evidence which points to the historical authenticity of the Hebrew Bible. It is plain, even upon superficial examination of this book, that it contains, beside the severest penalties for sin, the most stinging accusations of infidelity against the people of God, and the most scorching rebukes of their crimes; it relates the transgressions of their kings and princes and priests; in short, it records everything which the Jewish nation and their rulers must have been anxious to keep silent, or to mitigate where it was necessary to write it down. Every reason of prudence and national self-love must have suggested to them to destroy such records where they existed, because they made their vaunted glory a story of everlasting shame. Compare this historical record of the Jewish people with the contemporary annals of the Assyrian, Persian, Greek, or Roman monarchs. These are full of extravagant laudations, of royal deeds of valor, of the splendor of their victories over other nations; whereas the statements of the Bible are simple, the narrative of heroic acts and signal divine favors is constantly mingled with incidents deeply self-humiliating for a race that called itself chosen of God above all the Gentiles. The

Jews record numerous defeats, shameful treacheries, and errors of their most beloved kings. They rebel, they commit every crime forbidden by the Law; yet whilst they kill the prophets who charge them with ingratitude, they patiently suffer the record of it all to go into the books which they know will be read to all the people for their shame. They make no attempt to minimize or to excuse themselves to their children, however much they love the glory of Israel and the splendor of Jerusalem as the one nation and city worthy of the most exalted patriotic praise. Other nations made themselves a religion in harmony with their passions, so as to soothe the conscience. But the Jew finds a law of life given him in the great book of Moses. He may fall from his ideals, he may worship idols, but he never ceases to recognize that this is wrong because it is contrary to the law of Jehovah.

IV.

THE STONES CRY OUT.

The chain of documentary and circumstantial evidence which points to the preservation, substantially intact, of the Bible as an historic record of the highest possible trustworthiness is completed by the daily increasing store of monuments which are brought to light, especially in Palestine, Assyria, and Egypt. Up to the middle of the present century the largest part of our knowledge of the ancient nations was drawn from the Bible. It was the one great treasure-house wherein the history of the East was to be found. We had Greek and Roman and some Egyptian historians, but their knowledge was confined to their own people, and needed to be supplemented by the details related in the Pentateuch, in Josue, Judges, Ruth, the two Books of Samuel, the Books of Kings, Paralipomenon, Esdras, Tobias, Judith, Esther, and the Machabees, all of which are historical books containing facts, statistics, constitutions, and dynastic lines, without which profane history would still be a doubtful and barren field of study.

But, lately, the studious industry of scholarly men has gone over the ground of the old events, to test with the instruments of historic criticism the veracity, and, incidentally, the authenticity of the Bible record. Aid-ed by the royal munificence of governments and private corporations, scholars went to search out and examine the monuments of antiquity in those parts where the Jewish race had dwelt during the periods recounted in the Bible. They found, mostly below the earth, and sometimes beneath the flood-beds of streams and lakes, traces in stone or clay or metal which pointed to their containing valuable information regarding the Persian, Assyrian, Egyptian, and other nations with whom the Hebrew people had come in contact. These traces were sometimes in signs and languages not understood or wholly unknown in our learned world, but with assiduous study the mysteries came, in course of time, to be unravelled. The story of these discoveries is in various ways extremely interesting, and we shall speak of them more in detail later on.

Besides the primitive inscriptions just referred to, a number of cities have been discovered which lay buried for many centuries beneath the ground upon which afterwards other races dwelt and built their homes. Excavations in Palestine go, day by day, to explain, where they do not simply corroborate, the statements of the Bible. The diggings about the supposed ancient site of Nineveh, in Babylonia, have unearthed the ruins of an immense library. Sir A. H. Layard, and subsequently Mr. George Smith and Hormuzd Rassam, have brought together a number of clay tablets which open an immense world of Assyrian and Babylonian literature, whose existence was hitherto known only by the indications given in the Book of Daniel and other historical portions of the Bible concerning the conquerors of the Jews. These discoveries, as Mr. A. H. Sayce remarks in his "Fresh Lights from Ancient Monuments" (page 17), have not only "shed a flood of light on the history and antiquity of the Old Testament, but they have served to illustrate and explain the language of the Old Testament as well."

The evidence brought to light by these monuments has left no doubt in the minds of scientific men as to the facts that occurred three and four thousand years ago. We read the inscriptions which bear witness to the work of the Chaldean king Nimrod, to Zoroaster the Elamite, to Khamu-rabi, the Arab of the days of Moses; we treasure as of primary historical importance the account of Herodotus, who visited Babylon at the time when Esdras and Nehemias, who were both ministers at the court of Artaxerxes, wrote their continuation of the Book of Chronicles for the Jewish brethren in Palestine. When we read the works of Tacitus and Suetonius, of Cicero and Virgil, all of whom indicate that they had some knowledge of the Jewish sacred books,[1] we entertain no doubt as to their existence or the authenticity of their writings; yet men under the guise of scientific criticism have sought to cast doubts upon the Biblical records which have in their favor a documentary evi-

[1] Cf. Hettinger-Bowden, "Revealed Religion," page 158.

dence a hundred times more accurate and trustworthy than any work of antiquity without exception in the whole range of history. If apologists were silent, the very stones would begin to cry out in behalf of the authenticity and antiquity of the Biblical records. Every day is bringing this truth into stronger relief. "Discovery after discovery," says Prof. Sayce, "has been pouring in upon us from Oriental lands, and the accounts given only ten years ago of the results of Oriental research are already beginning to be antiquated. ... The ancient world has been reawakened to life by the spade of the explorer and the patient skill of the decipherer, and we now find ourselves in the presence of monuments which bear the names or recount the deeds of the heroes of Scripture."

V.
HEAVENLY DOCTRINE.

"Whence but from heaven could men, unskilled in arts,
In several ages born, in several parts,
Weave such agreeing truths?"
(Dryden, *Religio Laici*.)

The Bible, regarded as a work of history which offers us proofs of credibility beyond those of any secular work of the same kind, has in its composition and style a refinement and loftiness of tone far superior to other writings of equal age which have come down to us. The Jews "attributed to these books, one and all of them, a character which at once distinguishes them from all other books, and caused the collection of them to be regarded in their eyes as one individual whole. This distinguishing character was the divine authority of every one of those books and of every part of every book."[1] This belief of the Jews was so strong, so universal, so unchanging that, as has already been said, it pervaded and regulated their entire religious, political, and social life during all the eventful centuries of Israelitish history.

That our Lord knew of this belief, that He endorsed it, preached and emphasized it repeatedly, is very evident from the authentic narrative of the Gospels. Expres-

[1] "The Sacred Scriptures," Humphrey.

sions indicating this are to be found everywhere in the writings of the evangelists: "Have you never read in the Scriptures?" He says to the Scribes in referring to the words of the Psalmist (cxvii. 22): The stone which the builders rejected, etc. (St. Matthew xxi. 42.) Again, a little later on, He charges the Sadducees who say there is no resurrection: "You err, not knowing the Scriptures" (Ibid. xxii. 29). In the Garden of Olives He bears witness to the prophetic character of the Book of Isaiah: "How then shall the Scriptures be fulfilled" (Ibid. xxvi. 54)? And the historian, a friend and Apostle of Christ, adds: "Now all this was done that the Scriptures of the prophets might be fulfilled" (Ibid. 56). St. John's Gospel, especially, abounds in references like the foregoing, which point to the intimate relation between the Messianic advent of Christ and the figures of the Old Law, and assure us that the books of the Prophets, as well as the accompanying historic accounts of the Scriptural books generally, were regarded as the sacred word of God, not only by the Jews, but by the disciples of Christ.

This sacred collection was generally spoken of as consisting of three parts, namely, the Law, the Prophets, and the Psalms. Philo and Josephus, both trained in the schools of the Pharisees, mention the division as one well understood among the Jews of their time. Christ Himself speaks of the Sacred Scriptures, in different places, with this same distinction.

Now the testimony of Christ, who proved Himself to be the Son of God, and therefore unerring truth, is explicit in so far as it appeals with a supreme and infallible authority to the Jewish Scriptures as to a testimony *not human, but divine.* " Have you not read that which was spoken *by God?* " He says, referring to the Mosaic Law in Exodus iii. 6 (St. Matt. xxii. 31). Many times He speaks of the Scriptures " that they may be fulfilled," thus indicating that they contain that which lay in the future, and whose foreknowledge must have come from God. This testimony of Our Lord is strengthened by the interpretation of His Apostles in the same sense.

Yet although the testimony of Christ and the Apostles regarding the fact that the Books of the Law and the Prophets and the Psalms are divinely inspired, is very explicit, we have nowhere a clear statement or a catalogue which might assure us what books and parts of books are actually comprised in this collection of the Sacred Scriptures of which our Lord speaks. Christ approves as the word of God those writings which were accepted as such among the Jews of His day, but He does not give us any definite security by this general endorsement that every chapter, every verse, much less every word of the Bible, as we have received it, is actually inspired. We are not therefore quite sure from the evidence thus far given that the Old Testament, as we have it, has in every part of it the sanction of Christ's testimony to its being truly the word of God. As to the New Testament, we know that, however accurate and trustworthy as a history of the times in which it was composed it may be, yet it could not have had the explicit approval of our Lord, simply because it had not been written and was not completed for about a hundred years after His death and glorious resurrection.

Yet we accept the New Testament as also inspired in just the same authoritative way as we receive the Hebrew writings of the Old Law. And nothing but a divine testimony, such as that of Christ, could assure us sufficiently that in the Sacred Scriptures we have the word of God.

What criterion have we by which to determine precisely what books and parts belong to this collection of Old Testament writings of which Christ speaks as the word of God? What authority have we, moreover, for believing the entire New Testament inspired, since it was written after the time of Christ? If Luther and other reformers, so-called, threw out some portions of the sacred text, by what standard or criterion were they guided? Some have answered that we need not the testimony of Christ or any other equally explicit proof to determine what parts belong to this collection of writings representing the inspired word of God. They hold, with Calvin, that a certain spiritual unction inherent in the Sacred Scriptures determines their source, and produces in the devout reader an interior sensation which gives him an absolute conviction of the truth. But common experience teaches that devout feelings may be produced by books which are not inspired, nay, by positively irreligious books, which appeal to our better sensitive nature in some passages whilst they destroy a proper regard for virtue in others. Moreover, the "absolute conviction of the truth" to be deduced from the reading of the Sacred Scriptures is belied by a similar experience, since various sects draw opposing conclusions from the same texts. As truth cannot contradict itself, and as Christ prayed that His followers all be of one mind, we do not feel safe in admitting mere subjective feeling and judgment as a test of what is God's word.

Therefore we must look for some other criterion. Indeed, if our Lord wished us to accept the Sacred Scriptures, including the New Testament, which was written many years after His time, and for a long time was known only to very much separated portions of the faithful, we may be quite sure that He provided a means, an authoritative and clear method, which would lead us to an unerring conclusion in regard to what is and what is not the inspired word of God. This would be all the more necessary for those who regard the Bible as the principal rule and source of their faith.

It is a well-established historical fact that Christ taught some "new doctrines," as they were called, and that He gave a commission to His followers, which they repeated and carried out at the sacrifice of their lives.

There is no obscurity whatever about certain words and precepts given by our Lord, historically recorded by six of His Apostles and by many of His disciples who had heard and seen Him, who honestly and intelligently believed in Him, and who were prepared to die, and in some cases actually did suffer martyrdom for the assertions they made. He bade them teach all nations the things He had taught them. He did not give them a book, as He might have done, nor did He tell them to write books; for some of the Apostles never wrote anything; and of those who did write in later days, some had actually never seen our Lord. Such is the common belief regarding St. Paul, who wrote more than any other of the evangelical writers. St. Luke, in the very opening of his Gospel, tells us that he wrote what had been delivered to him by those who were eye-witnesses and ministers of the word. Our Lord did not, therefore, give His disciples a book, but He was very explicit in making them understand and feel that He gave them an unerring Spirit, who would be just the same as Himself, verily identical with their living Master and Teacher, Christ, who would abide with them to the end of time. *" Behold, I am with you all days, even to the consummation of the world."* To the consummation of the world? And were they never to die? Were they actually to go, as some believed of St. John, to perpetuate the kingdom of Christ, wandering over the earth until all the nations were converted? Not so. They were to deliver His doctrine to their successors, and the Holy Spirit, the Paraclete, would watch over it until the end of ages. St. Peter would live, in this sense, forever, and all the opposing forces of error, the mighty gates of hell, would not overcome that Spirit any more than they would triumph over Christ, who had "overcome the world." To St. Peter He said: "To thee I give the keys of the kingdom of heaven;" "Confirm thou thy brethren." All this was to go on and on, so that every human creature could come into possession of truth through this unerring Spirit that presided over the Christian doctrine. And this perpetual transmission of the Holy Spirit, the Spirit of Truth, who would guide the future teachers and preside over their councils as at the first councils of Antioch and Jerusalem,—this perpetual transmission through a body like the apostolic body, ever living, ever guarded from error, ever triumphant amid humiliations, what else is it but the Church, that glorious heritage of ages, which we recognize through all time in every land, holding every class and condition with the wondrous power of its unity of doctrine and discipline!

Now it is this body, this ever-living and unchanging organism, this grand apostolic tribunal, which Christ established, and without which His mission to men would really have remained incomplete, that tells us that the things which some of the Apostles and some of the disciples wrote for our instruction and edification are inspired by the same holy and infallible Spirit which guided the Apostles in their oral teaching. Not all things were written there, as St. John tells us, but many things which they had taught, and which would keep the people, with whom the Apostles could not be ever present, in mind of that doctrine. The written things were not intended to replace the spoken word of doctrinal jurisdiction, for the evangelical teaching of the spoken word was to go on to the end; besides, there were many who could not read, and many who might listen but would not read. Futhermore, there would be need of a living apostolic tribunal, since a written doctrine, like a written law, is liable to various and sometimes contradictory interpretations. We have constitutions and laws, but we need judges and courts to decide the meaning and application, and if it were not that men forget the order of justice, or are too remote from the centres of jurisdiction, we should not need any written laws at all. Communities may be governed by a wise superior without any written laws, and in no case does the written law dispense with the necessity of a discretionary living authority. It is quite evident that in the matter of truth God wished His Apostles to use *all the instruments* by which that truth might be safely and rightly communicated, and thus the written word was added to the living teaching which the Holy Ghost was ever to direct and safeguard.

I repeat: Christ did not give His disciples a book, but a living, infallible spirit, abiding with them to the end of time, as He said; and since the Apostles were not to remain on earth to the end of the world, what else could our Lord have meant but that others would take their place on the same conditions, with the same prerogatives! That He wished and said this is written over and over again in the sacred volume, and by men who, if they had held this grand trust only for themselves, would have had every reason to say so. But they state the contrary. St. Peter ordains St. Paul; St. Paul sends Timothy and Titus to the new converts on the same conditions, bidding them to preserve intact the grace that is in them "through the imposition of hands." And the successive generations of Pontiffs who take the place of Peter and Paul and Timothy and Titus are the grand tribunal for the transmission of Christ's doctrine.

That tribunal, from St. Peter down to Leo XIII., is the authority: "Christ having sent them, even as the Father had sent Him," which tells us that the books of the Sacred Scriptures, such as we have them, and as they are singly defined in what is called the Catholic Canon of Biblical Books, are truly and really the word of God, and were written under the impulsion of the Holy Spirit.

VI.

THE VICIOUS CIRCLE.

In the preceding chapter it was said that the Sacred Scripture of the New Testament contains Christ's statements according to which He founded an ever-living tribunal of doctrine which decided the question of what books are, and what books are not inspired, whenever there is any doubt about such books. Perhaps you will say: "But is this not arguing in a circle—a vicious circle, as philosophers say? You prove the existence of the Church as the tribunal to determine what books belong to the Sacred Scriptures from the words of the Bible; and then you turn about and prove the inspiration of the Bible from the authority of the Church." Now mark the difference. When in my first argument I refer to the Bible as containing Christ's statement and the commission given to His Apostles, I am taking the testimony of the Bible, not as an inspired or divine book, but simply as a trustworthy historical record which tells us the fact, repeated by several eye-witnesses and sincere men, such as the evangelists and apostolical writers, that Christ, of whose divinity they were convinced, had said and emphasized the fact that He meant to found a Church. And as that Church was to have the divine spirit abiding in it, guiding its decisions, it came naturally within the province of that Church to define whether certain books were to be regarded as really inspired by that Holy Spirit. Thus the Church placed upon these books the mark and sign-manual of that commission which she had unquestionably received.

But I am constrained, for the sake of completing our present aspect of the subject, to say something on the character and extent of that divine element which Jews and Christians recognize when they accept the Sacred Scriptures as the word of God.

VII.

THE SACRED PEN.

We have seen that the Biblical writings bear the unmistakable impress of a divine purpose. The nature of that purpose is likewise clearly enunciated on every page of Holy Writ. Man in his fallen condition stands in need of law and example, of precept and promise. These God gives him. We read in Exodus (Chap. iii.) that He first speaks to Moses, giving him His commands regarding the liberation and conduct of His people out of Egypt. Later on, in the desert on Mount Sinai, " Moses spoke, and God answered him " (Chap. xix. 19); and " Moses went down to the people and told them all " (Ibid. 25). Next we read (Chap. xxiv. 12) that the Lord said to Moses: " I will give thee tables of stone, and the law, and the commandments which *I have written, that thou mayest teach them.*"

Here God announces Himself as the writer of "the Law and the Commandments," although we receive them in the handwriting of Moses. Is Moses a mere amanuensis, writing under dictation? No. He is the intelligent, free instrument, writing under the direct inspiration of God. In this sense God is the true author or writer of the Sacred Scriptures, making His action plain to the sense and understanding of His children through the medium of a man whom He inspires to execute His work.

How does this inspiration act on the writer who ostensibly executes the divine work? We answer: *God moves the will of the writer, and illumines his intellect, pointing out to him at the same time the subject-matter which he is to write down, and preserving him from error in the completion of his committed task.*

Looking attentively at this definition of Scriptural inspiration, a number of questions arise at once in our minds. God moves the will, enlightens the mind, and points out the subject-matter which the inspired writer commits to paper. Is the writer under the influence of the divine impulsion so possessed by the inspired virtue that he acts without any freedom, either as regards the manner of his expression or the use of previously acquired knowledge concerning the subject of which he writes?

I answer: No. God moves the will of the writer; He does not annihilate it or absorb it, unless in the sense that He brings it, by a certain illumination of the intellect, to a conformity with His own. Hence the manner and method of expression retain the traces of the individuality of the writer, that is to say, of his views and feelings as determined by the ordinary habits of life and the range of his previous knowledge. The idea of the divine authorship of the Sacred Scriptures by no means requires that the truths which God willed to be contained therein could not or should not have been otherwise known to the inspired writers: "Their use of study, their investigation of documents, their interrogation of witnesses and other evidence, and their excuses for rusticity of style and poverty of language show this only, that they were not inanimate, but living, intelligent, and rational instruments—that they were men, and not machines. ... They were employed in a manner which corresponded to, and which became the nature, the mode, and the conditions of their being. Previous knowledge of certain truths by men can be no reason why God should not conceive and will such truths to be communicated by means of Scripture to His Church. ... Hence the idea of inspiration does not exclude human industry, study, the use of documents and witnesses, and other aids in order to the conceiving of such truths, so long as it includes a supernatural operation and direction of God, which effects that the mind of the inspired writer should *conceive* all those truths, and those only which God would have him communicate."[1] And herein lies the difference between inspiration and revelation, the latter being the manifestation of something previously unknown to the writer.

The second question, which naturally occurs in connection with the one just answered, is whether we are to consider that the words, just as we read them in the Bible, are inspired in such wise that we may not conceive of the sacred text having any other meaning than that to which its *verbal expression* limits it.

There are many reasons why we need not feel bound to accept the theory of literal or *verbal inspiration* of the Bible, although such opinion has been defended by eminent theologians, who wished thereby to defend the integrity of the sacred volume against the wanton interference with the received text on the part of innovators and so-called religious reformers.

In the first place, the theory of verbal inspiration is not essential to the maintenance of the absolute integrity of a written revelation. That revelation proposes truths and facts, and whilst the terms employed for the expression of these truths and facts must fit adequately to convey the sense, they admit of a certain variety without thereby in the least injuring the accuracy of statements. This is applicable not only to single words,

---

[1] Vid. "The Sacred Scriptures; or, The Written Word of God." By William Humphrey, S. J.—London, Art and Book Co., 1894.

but to phrases and forms of diction, and to figures of illustration.

Secondly, the sacred writers themselves abundantly indicate the freedom which may be exercised or allowed in the verbal declaration of divinely inspired truths. Many of them repeat the same facts and doctrines in different words. This is the case even with regard to events of the gravest character, such as the institution of the Blessed Eucharist, in which there can be no room for a difference of interpretation as to the true sense.

St. Matthew (xxvi. 26-28), for example, records the act of consecration by our Lord on the eve of His passion in the following words: "Take ye and eat: This is My Body. ... Drink ye all of this, for this is My Blood of the new Testament, which shall be shed for many for the remission of sins."

St. Mark (xiv. 22-24) writes: "Take ye. This is My Body. ... This is My Blood of the new Testament, which shall be shed for many."

St. Luke (xxii. 19-20) says: "This is My Body, which is given for you. ... This is the chalice, the new Testament in My Blood, which shall be shed for you."

St. Paul (I. Cor. xi. 24-25) has it: "This is My Body, which shall be delivered for you. ... This chalice is the new Testament in My Blood."

These four witnesses cite very important words spoken by our Lord on a most solemn occasion. St. Matthew was present at the Last Supper. He wrote in the very language employed by our Lord, and we have every reason to believe that he could remember and wished to remember exactly what our Lord had said on so important a subject, especially when he, with the other Apostles, was told to do the same act in remembrance of their Master when He should be no longer with them in visible human form. St. Mark, St. Luke, and St. Paul nevertheless vary the expression of this tremendous mystery in all but the words: "This is My Body." They drew their knowledge of the form of the institution of the Blessed Sacrament from St. Peter; at least we know that St. Peter revised and approved of St. Mark's Gospel,[1] and St. Paul and St. Luke evidently obtained their knowledge of the Christian faith from a common source, which the chief of the Apostles controlled. They had every opportunity to consult St. Mark, and there might have been reason for doing so since they wrote in Greek, whereas St. Matthew retained the Hebrew idiom, but evidently neither they nor St. Peter deemed a literal or verbal rendering of the sacramental form essential, provided the true version of our Lord's action was faithfully given.

Furthermore, the claim of verbal inspiration implies a necessity of having recourse to the original language in which the inspired writers composed their works,

---

[1] Clement Alex.—Euseb., H. E., II. xv. 1; VI. xiv. 6; XX. clxxii. 552. Also Hieron., De Vir. Ill., VIII. xxiii. 621, etc.

since it is quite impossible that translations can in every case adequately render the exact meaning conveyed by an idiom no longer living. But the necessity of referring to the Hebrew, Chaldee, or Greek text in order to verify the true sense of an expression would place the Bible beyond the reach of all but a few scholars, for whose exclusive benefit the generally popular style of the Bible forbids us to think they were primarily intended.

Finally, we have the indication by writers of both the Old and New Testaments that what they wrote was not conveyed to them by way of dictation, but that the divine thought conceived in their own minds was rendered by them with such imperfections of expression as belonged wholly to the human element of the instrument which God employed, and could in nowise be attributed to the Holy Ghost, who permitted His revelation to be communicated through channels of various kinds and degrees of material form. Thus the writer of the sacred Book of Machabees (II. Mach. ii. 24, etc.) apologizes for his style of writing. St. Paul (I. Cor. ii. 13; II. Cor. xi. 6) gives us to understand that his words fall short of the requirements of the rhetorician, but that he is satisfied to convey "the doctrine of the Spirit."

VIII.

THE MELODY AND HARMONY OF THE "VOX CŒLESTIS."

But, you will say, whilst it is plain that we need not adhere to the text of Holy Writ so strictly as to suppose that each single word is the only exact representation of the thought or truth with which God inspired the writer, it seems difficult to see where you can draw the line between the teaching of God and its interpretation by man who is not bound by definite words. In other words, if verbal inspiration is not to be admitted, how far does inspiration actually extend in the formation of the written text?

I should answer that inspiration extends to the *truths* and *facts* contained in the Bible, *absolutely;* that it extends to the terms in which these truths and facts are expressed, *relatively*. The former cannot vary; the latter may vary according to the disposition or the circumstances of the writer. It may be allowable to express this distinction by a comparison of Biblical with musical inspiration. Taking music, not as a mechanical art, but as an expression of the soul, or, as Milton puts it, of

"Strains that might create a soul,"

we distinguish between the conception of the melody and its accompaniment of harmonious chords. The former constitutes, so to speak, the theme, the truth, or motive of the artistic conception, which the composer seizes under his inspiration. When he goes to communicate the expression of this musical truth or melody through the instrument he at once and instinctively avails himself of the chords which, by way of accompaniment, emphasize the musical truth which his soul utters through the instrument, according to the peculiar nature or form of the latter. These chords of the accompaniment are not the leading motive or truth of his theme, but they are equally true with it. They may vary, even whilst he uses the same instrument, but the melody must ever observe the exact distances between the sounds in its finished form, and cannot be altered without changing the motive of the piece.

The inspiration of the Sacred Text offers an analogy to that of the artist musician. The divine melody of truths and facts is definitely communicated to the inspired composer of the Sacred Books. Sometimes he sings loud and with strong emphasis, sometimes he barely breathes his heavenly tones, yet they are no uncertain notes; they allow of no alteration, addition, or omission. But in the accompanying chords he takes now one set, now another, remaining in the same clef, ever true to the melody, yet manifold in the variety of expressing that truth. Even the seeming discords, which, taken by themselves, look like errors, prove to be part of the great theme; when rightly understood they are but transition chords which prepare us for the complete realization of the succeeding harmony into which they resolve themselves.

IX.

THE VOICE FROM THE ROCK.

Does the Church indorse the definition of Scriptural inspiration which has been given in the two preceding chapters? The Church has said very little on the subject of the inspiration of the Sacred Scriptures, but enough to serve us as a definition and as an expression of its limitations. The Councils of Florence and Trent simply state that "the Sacred Scriptures, having been written under the inspiration of the Holy Ghost, have God for their author." How much may be deduced from this was made clear by the late Vatican Council (Constit., *de Fide,* cap. ii.), which holds that "the Church regards these books (enumerated in the Tridentine Canon), as sacred and canonical, not because, having been composed through the care and industry of men, they were afterwards approved by the authority of the Church, nor simply because they contain revealed truth without error, but because they were written under the inspiration of the Holy Ghost in such a way as to have God for their author. ..."[1]

---

[1] See on this subject P. Brucker's recently published work "*Questions Actuelles d'Ecriture Sainte,*" par le R. P. Jos. Brucker, S. J.: Paris, Victor Retaux, which treats admirably this part of our subject.

By this definition two distinct theories of inspiration are censured as contrary to Catholic teaching. The first is that which has been called *subsequent* inspiration, according to which a book might be written wholly through human industry, but receiving afterwards the testimony of express divine approval, might become the written word of God. This teaching is not admissible inasmuch as it excludes the divine authorship of the Scriptures.

A second theory condemned by the above clause of the Vatican Council as untenable on Catholic principles is that which is called *negative* inspiration. Its defenders hold that the extent of the divine action in the composition of the Sacred Scriptures is limited to the exclusion of errors from the sacred volume. This would restrict the value of the truth revealed in the Bible to a mere exposition of human knowledge containing no actual misstatements of fact.

X.

A SOURCE OF GENERAL INFORMATION AND CULTURE.

Among the many interesting letters which St. Jerome has left us there is one to Laeta, a noble lady of Rome, regarding the education of her little daughter, Paula. An aunt of the child was at the time in Bethlehem, where, amid the very scenes where our Lord was born, she studied the Holy Scriptures in the Hebrew and Greek tongues, as was then the habit of educated Christian ladies. St. Jerome would have the child Paula trained in all the arts and sciences that could refine her mind and lead it to its highest exercise in that singularly gifted nature. To this end he bids Laeta cultivate in the child an early knowledge of the Sacred Scriptures. With a touching simplicity the aged Saint enters into minute details of the daily training,—how the childish hands are to form the ivory letters, which serve her as playthings, into the names of the prophets and saints of the Old Testament; how later she is to commit to memory, each day, choice sayings, flowers of wisdom culled from the sacred writers, and how, finally, he is to come to the Holy Land and learn from her aunt the lofty erudition and understanding of the Bible, a book which contains and unfolds to him who knows how

A Source of General Information and Culture. 53

to read it rightly all the wisdom of ages, practical and in principle, surpassing the classic beauty of those renowned Roman writers of whose works St. Jerome himself had been once so passionately fond that they haunted him in his dreams.

It must not be supposed, however, that the judgment of so erudite a man as St. Jerome in placing the study of the Sacred Scriptures above all other branches of a higher education was based upon a purely *spiritual* view. He realized what escapes the superficial reader of the inspired writings: that they are *not only* a library of religious thought, but, in every truest sense of the word, a compendium of general knowledge. The sacred volumes are a code and digest of law, of political, social, and domestic economy; a book of history the most comprehensive and best authenticated of all written records back to the remotest ages; a summary of practical lessons and maxims for every sphere of life; a treasury of beautiful thoughts and reflections, which instruct at once and elevate, and thus serve as a most effective means of education. That this is no exaggeration is attested by men like the pagans of old, who, becoming acquainted with the sacred books, valued them, though they saw in them nothing of that special divine revelation which the Jew and Christian recognize. We read in history how, nearly three hundred years before our Lord, Ptolemy Philadelphus, the most cultured of all the Egyptian kings, and founder of the famous Alexandrian University, which for centuries outshone every other institution of learning by the renown of its teachers, sent a magnificent embassy to the High-priest Eleazar at Jerusalem to ask him for a copy of the Sacred Law of the Jews. So greatly did he esteem its possession that he offered for the right of translating the Pentateuch alone six hundred talents of gold ($576,-000), and liberty to all the Jewish captives in his dominion, to the number of about 150,000 (some historians give the number at 100,000, others at 200,000).

There exists a spurious account, ascribed to Aristeas, one of Ptolemy's ministers, who is said to have accompanied the royal embassy to Jerusalem for the purpose of urging the king's request. According to this story, which is in form of a letter written by Aristeas to his brother Philocrates, six rabbis, equally well versed in the Hebrew and Greek languages, were selected by the high-priest from each of the twelve tribes. The seventy-two rabbis were invited to the palace of the king, who, whilst entertaining them for some time, publicly asked them questions relating to civil government and moral philosophy, so that by this means he might test their knowledge and judgment. Many of these questions, curious and quaint, have been preserved, and are intended to show the wisdom of Ptolemy and his desire to raise his government to a high level of moral and political perfection. Among the guests who were present at the king's table we find Demetrius Phalereus, the famous librarian, Euclid, the mathematician, Theocritus, the Greek poet philosopher, and Manetho, the Egyptian historian, together with other equally learned and illustrious scholars and literary artists.

Later on the seventy-two translators, according to the same tradition, which has come to us through some of the old ecclesiastical writers, were brought to the island of Pharos, where they went to work in separate cells, undisturbed and living according to a uniform rule, until the entire work of translation had been accomplished. Then the results were compared, and it was found that the translations of all agreed in a wonderful manner, and the Jews accepted it as a work done under the special protection of Jehovah.

Whatever we may hold as to the accuracy of the above account and its pretended origin, it is certain that the story was current before the time of Christ, it being credited by Philo, who repeats it in his Life of Moses, and by Josephus, as well as by St. Justin Martyr and others of the early Christian Fathers. All agree that the Septuagint translation was made about the time of Ptolemy, and that the Jews of Alexandria and Palestine held it in equal veneration as a faithful copy of the Mosaic books, whilst the pagans regarded it in the light of a wonderfully complete code of laws—civil, domestic, and moral.

Reference has already been made to the Sacred Scriptures as constituting the oldest and best-authenticated record of ancient history. From it we draw the main store of our information regarding the beginnings of human society in the Eastern countries of Mesopotamia, early Chaldea, Assyria, Persia, Arabia, and Egypt, all of which are grouped around the common centre, Palestine, where the principal scenes of the Old and New Testament narrative are laid.

But it is not only in the departments of history and geography that the Bible represents the most extensive and reliable source of information hitherto open to the student of mental culture. The sacred books, although never intended to serve a purely scientific purpose, have within recent years become recognized indicators which throw light upon doubtful paths in the investigation of certain scientific facts. Sir William Dawson, one of the leading investigators of our day, has lately published his Lowell lectures, in which he shows how science at last confirms and illustrates the teaching of Holy Writ regarding geology and the creation of man.[1] Similar conclusions are being daily reached in different fields of scientific research, and the words of Jean Paul regarding the first page of the Mosaic record, as containing more real knowledge than all the folios of men of science and philosophy, are proving themselves true in other respects also. We may be allowed to cite here from Geikie's "Hours With the Bible" the testimony of the late Dr.

[1] "Meeting-place of Geology and History," 1894. Fleming H. Revell Co., New York.

McCaul, who gives us a legitimate view of the latest results of science as compared with the Mosaic record of the Bible.

"Moses," he says, "relates how God created the heavens and the earth at an indefinitely remote period, before the earth was the habitation of man: Geology has lately discovered the existence of a long prehuman period. A comparison with other Scriptures (*i. e.*, those written after the Pentateuch, or Mosaic account) shows that the "heavens" of Moses include the abode of angels and the place of the fixed stars, which existed before the earth: Astronomy points out remote worlds, whose light began its journey long before the existence of man. Moses declares that the earth was or became covered with water, and was desolate and empty: Geology has found by investigation that the primitive globe was covered with a uniform ocean, and that there was a long azoic period, during which neither plant nor animal could live. Moses states that there was a time when the earth was not dependent on the sun for light or heat; when, therefore, there could be no climatic differences: Geology has lately verifed this statement by finding tropical plants and animals scattered over all places of the earth. Moses affirms that the sun, as well as the moon, is only a light holder: Astronomy declares that the sun is a non-luminous body, dependent for its light on a luminous atmosphere. Moses asserts that the earth existed before the sun was given as a luminary: Modern science proposes a theory which explains how this was possible. Moses asserts that there is an expanse extending from earth to distant heights, in which the heavenly bodies are placed: Recent discoveries lead to the supposition of some subtile fluid medium in which they move. Moses describes the process of creation as gradual, and mentions the order in which living things appeared: plants, fishes, fowls, land animals, man: By the study of nature, geology has arrived independently at the same conclusion. Whence did Moses get all this knowledge? How was it that he worded his rapid sketch with such scientific accuracy? If he in his day possessed the knowledge which genius and science have attained only recently, that knowledge is superhuman. If he did not possess the knowledge, then his pen must have been guided by superhuman wisdom" (Aids to Faith, p. 232).

Some years ago much ado was made by certain sceptics about the chronology of the Bible, as if the discrepancies of a few figures could undo the manifest authenticity of the vast store of facts vouched in the grand collection of Biblical books. These discrepancies are being gradually explained. It may be that we err in properly understanding the Oriental habits of counting genealogies, or that the method of the first transcribers led to inaccuracy, despite the care used in the copying and preservation of the text. When we remember that Hebrew signs, very closely resembling each other, denote often great differences, clear enough, no doubt, at first,

A Source of General Information and Culture. 59

but becoming indistinct in the course of time, we cannot wonder that some words and expressions present to the ordinary reader a mystery, or even seeming contradiction. It is not necessary to understand the ancient tongue in order to realize this fact. In the first place, the similarity of Hebrew characters which represent great numerical differences must have easily led to errors by the copyists, which caused difficulty to the later transcribers unless they had a reliable tradition to correct the mistake. Thus the letter ב (*Beth*) represents *two*, whilst כ (*Kaph*) represents *twenty*. By placing two small dots above either of these two characters you multiply them by a thousand, ב̈ representing *two thousand* and כ̈ *twenty thousand*. The letter ו (*Vav*) is equivalent to *six*, another letter very like it in form, ז (*Zayin*), is *seven*, whilst both of these characters represent a variety of meanings: oftenest ו (*Vav*) is a copula, at other times it stands at the beginning of a discourse, or introduces the apodosis, or is simply an intensive, or adversative; sometimes it is prefixed to a future tense, and turns it into an imperfect, etc. Again, there are special reasons why certain combinations of letters stand for numerals, contrary to the ordinary rule. Thus *fifteen* is expressed by טו=9+6, instead of יה, because the name of God commences with the latter characters יהוה (Jehovah), etc.

Furthermore, many of the signs used as numerals had fixed symbolical significations, and were not meant to be taken as literal quantities.

Moreover, in all the old Hebrew writings the consonants only are expressed. Thus it happens that the same written characters may denote different things, sometimes contradictory, unless living tradition could supply the true signification. Thus the word בר means *son* (Ps. ii. 12), or it may be an adjective signifying *chosen* (Cant. vi. 9), or, again, *clear* (Cant. vi. 10), or *empty* (Prov. xiv. 4). Besides these primary meanings it stands for *corn* or *grain*, for *open fields* or *country*, for a *pit*, for *salt of lye* (vegetable salt), and for *pureness*. The true signification in each passage is not always clear from the context, and critics are frequently at a loss to divine the sense intended by the writer.

But whilst these discrepancies and obscurities are a momentary source of distraction, they arouse not only zeal for the study of the sacred languages, by which means philological mysteries are frequently cleared up, but they give us often an insight into the wonderful genius of the Semitic languages, with their peculiar imagery, which associates ideas and feelings apparently wholly distinct from each other according to the use of modern terms.

The last-made reflection suggests another advantage, in an educational point of view, which the study of the Sacred Scriptures opens to those who possess sufficient talent and opportunity for its pursuit. I mean the power of thought and reflection which comes with the study of a foreign language. There are portions of the

Old Testament which we cannot rightly read and understand without *some* knowledge of the tongue in which they were originally written. This is one of the several reasons which the Church has for not sanctioning, without certain cautions, the indiscriminate reading of the Sacred Scriptures in the form of translation. Let me give you a very good authority for this.

About the very time when Ptolemy Philadelphus, of whom I have spoken in the beginning, sent to Jerusalem in order to procure the Greek translation of the Thorah, or Hebrew law (Pentateuch), a holy Jewish scribe was inspired to write one of the later Scriptural books. It appears that he was among the seventy learned scribes who had been sent by the High-priest to Alexandria for the purpose of making the translation for the king, and that afterwards, whilst still there, he composed the sacred book known as *Ecclesiasticus*. This book he wrote in the Hebrew tongue. Many years after, a grandson of this inspired writer, who is called Jesus son of Sirach, came upon the book and resolved to translate it into Greek, in order that it might be read by many of his brethren in the foreign land, who no longer spoke the Hebrew language, though they believed in the law of their forefathers. To this translation he wrote a short preface which, though it does not belong to the inspired portions of the text, has been preserved and is found in our Bibles. Let me read it to you, because it demonstrates the truth of what I have just said, namely, that our understanding of the Bible is rendered difficult when we are obliged to depart from the original language in which it was written. The younger Jesus Sirach, who spoke both the Hebrew and Greek tongues equally well, at a time when they were still living languages, writes as follows about the translation of his grandfather's work:

"The knowledge of many and great things hath been shown us by the Law and the Prophets, and others that have followed them, for which things Israel is to be commended for doctrine and wisdom; because not only they that speak must needs be skilful, but strangers also, both speaking and writing, may by their means become most learned.

My grandfather Jesus, after he had much given himself to a diligent reading of the Law and the Prophets, and other books that were delivered to us from our fathers, had a mind also to write something himself pertaining to doctrine and wisdom; that such as are desirous to learn and are made knowing in these things may be more and more attentive in mind, and be strengthened to live according to the Law. I entreat you, therefore, to come with benevolence, and to read with attention, and to pardon us for those things wherein we may seem, *while we follow the image of wisdom, to come short in the composition of words: for the Hebrew words have not the same force in them when translated into another tongue. And not only these, but the Law also itself, and the Prophets and the rest of the books, have no small difference when they are spoken in their own language.* For in the eighth and thirtieth year coming into Egypt, when Ptolemy Euergetes was king, and continuing there a long time, I found these books left, of no small and contemptible learning. Therefore I thought it good and necessary for me to bestow some diligence and labor to interpret this book; and with much watching and study, in some space of time, I brought the book to an end, and set it forth for the service of them that are willing to apply their mind, and to learn how they ought to conduct themselves, who purpose to lead their life according to the Law of the Lord " (Prologue to Ecclesiasticus).

XI.

THE CREATION OF NEW LETTERS.

It is a fact not generally known or realized that if it were not for the Bible some of the richest and most beautiful languages of antiquity would now be entirely lost to us; nay, more, there are whole nations who would in all probability never have had a written language or literature except for the Bible.

Of the ancient Semitic tongues only two remain living languages, that is, the Arabian, and, in a modified form, the Syrian. The Chaldee, the Samaritan, the Assyrian, the Phœnician, the Ethiopic are dead and would hardly be known to us except for the remnants of them which we trace through the sacred books of the Scripture. We have no relic of the Hebrew tongue but the Bible; and this language, with all its wondrous musical forms, its strange capacity of eliciting and expressing the deepest feelings of the human heart, and its charming touches of Oriental genius, would be entirely dead outs, if we had not the Bible.

Our own English tongue bears the traces of another written language, now entirely dead, but which was actually created by the study of the Bible. I mean the Gothic, of which no other written document exists to-day except some portion of the Holy Scriptures translated by Ulfilas in the fourth century. When he came as a missionary among the Goths he found them ignorant of the art of writing. In order to Christianize the rude people he invented for them an alphabet, gathered their children into Christian schools, and taught them to write and to read. The first book, and the last, too, of that once powerful race was a Bible. When the Goths had died out in the ninth century, their written copy of the inspired word of God still continued to live, and we can trace in our unabridged dictionaries to-day the original meaning of many a Saxon word by reference to this solitary copy of a part of the Sacred Scriptures.

What has been said of the Gothic is equally true of the written language of the Armenians (for whom the anchorite Miesrop devised an alphabet and translated the Bible); also of the Slavonic nations (for whom SS. Cyril and Methodius made an alphabet and Bible translation); and others—races who, like our own Indian tribes, lived only long enough as representatives of a separate language to learn the rudiments of Christianity.

All this must convince us that those who have the required means should seek to master one or several of the Biblical languages, since the ancient tongues, less subject to the caprice of political changes than those of later ages, open to the mind avenues of original thought and sentiment which modern literature and education have not been capable of retaining without them.

You will say that it is impossible for most, or perchance nearly all of you to give yourselves to the study of Hebrew or Greek or Latin in order to gain that profit from the intelligent reading of the Bible which it yields to the man of learning. Very well; if so, the fact of our deficiency must caution us in reading and rashly interpreting according to our fancy what can only be determined by the wisdom of those who act the legitimate part of divinely-appointed judges. As in the Old Law the High-priest and the great council of the Sanhedrin were the infallible interpreters of the divine decrees, so the Church, which is the continuation and perfection of the Synagogue, completes the Messianic mission by interpreting for each succeeding generation the meaning of the inspired words written in the sacred volume.

XII.

ENGLISH STYLE.

But there still remains for all of us the reading of the English Bible, with the aids of interpretation which render it intelligible for a practical purpose, and in so far as it is an expression of the natural moral law. This of itself contributes very largely to the perfection of our use of the mother tongue. For it is always true of this sacred book, as Dryden says, that in

> "... Style, majestic and divine,
> It speaks no less than God in every line;
> Commanding words! whose force is still the same
> As the first *fiat* that produced our frame."
> (Dryden, *Relig. Laic.*, i. 152.)

Yes, its frequent reading helps much to the formation of good English. This is not simply fancy, but the verdict of those who have experienced and proved the benefit of frequent use of the Bible as a means of fashioning and improving a beautiful style of English writing. Some years ago Mr. Bainton, a lover of English literature, requested the best of living writers to give their opinion as to what class of reading had most contributed to their attaining the elegance or force of beauty for which their writings were generally admired. To the surprise of many it appeared in the answers that the

English Style. 67

reading of the Bible was considered the secret of a charming style, even by authors who wrote in that lighter, sparkling vein which seems so remote from the gravity and solidity of the sacred books. To give one example of this let me quote the words of Mr. W. S. Gilbert, the author of the delightful " Bab Ballads," and a long series of light operas and sparkling plays. After referring to the advantage of studying the English of the late Tudor and early Stuart periods, he adds: " But for simplicity, directness, and perspicuity, there is, in my opinion, no existing work to be compared with the historical books of the Bible."

Mr. Marion Crawford, much read of late, and criticized for fostering a faulty ideal, but whose vigorous expression, power of analysis, and correct delineation of character will hardly be denied by any one capable of judging, gives his ideas of attaining to good English style in the following words: "The greatest literary production in our language is the translation of the Bible, and the more a man reads it the better he will write English." He adds: " I am not a particularly devout person, though I am a good Roman Catholic, and I do not recommend the Bible from any religious reason. I distinctly dislike the practice of learning texts without any regard to the context. ... But if we were English Brahmans, and believed nothing contained therein, I should still maintain that the Bible should be the *first study* of a literary man. Then the great poets,

Shakespeare, Milton," etc. I have quoted Mr. Crawford because he is not merely a good English writer, but a real scholar, familiar with many languages, classic and modern, and therefore all the better qualified to judge of our subject.

There are, of course, instances in the Bible when the grammatical rules of Brown and Murray forbid satisfactory parsing. The reason of this is the natural wish of the translators, anxious to preserve the literal form of the original, not to sacrifice accuracy to the nicety with which they might round their phrases. They were intent alone upon truth; and it is precisely in this element that eloquence finds its first and most powerful incentive. Beauty of language has two sources of inspiration. One is that of truth, which arouses in the heart a love lifting the mind with a burning enthusiasm into the regions of all that is fair and chaste and grand; and the language of him who has mastered it assumes the sound and form of these lofty emotions. There is indeed another source of inspiration. It is that from which emanates the brilliant but ephemeral beauty of the literature of the day. It is not love of unchanging truth, but the captivating passion of the hour, which, as some one has said, acts upon the brain "like the foaming grape of Eastern France—pleasant to the sense of taste, yet sending its subtle fumes to the brain, and stealing away the judgment." Truth in literature possesses a power of eloquence of which fiction is but a shadow at best, varying in size, and dwarfed or magnified in proportion as it approaches and recedes from the object which occasions it.

XIII.

FRIENDS OF GOD.

And with this study of truth there is added to knowledge and power and beauty of expression another vital element, which gives these acquisitions an infinite value: I mean the gift of wisdom as distinct from knowledge. Read the Sapiential book of Solomon, and mark what he there says. He had learnt all things that human industry could suggest, but the science of things earthly was as nothing to the wisdom which, as he says, "went before me; and I knew not that it was the mother of all." And when he had learnt wisdom in listening to the breathing of that sacred voice whose words he recorded for our instruction, he describes it as a sacred fire of genius, "holy, one, manifold, subtle, eloquent, active, undefiled, sure, sweet, loving that which is good, quick, which nothing can oppose, beneficent, gentle, kind, steadfast, assured—a breath of the power of God —making friends of God, and prophets, for God loveth none but him that dwelleth with wisdom—more beautiful than the sun" (Sap. vii. 22-29).

Surely, it makes us friends of God and prophets. But not only this. It keeps high ideals before us, and we become like to the things we love. Look on Abraham, whom the Arab calls even to this day by no other name but *El Khalil Allah*—that is, "the friend of God"—chosen the father of a holy race whence eventually was to spring the Messias; look on Moses, the meekest of men, as he is called in Holy Writ, or on David, the man "according to God's own heart;" look on the later prophets, whose words set the nations aflame, and made kings tremble who had never felt fear of men or God. We see Jeremiah, the youth at Anathoth, "gentle, sensitive, yielding, yearning for peace and love, averse by nature from strife and controversy," stepping forth at the urging of motives such as speak to each of us from these pages of the Bible. Boldly he announces the judgments of God to his faithless people. "During that long ministry" of forty years, says Geikie, " no personal interest, comfort, or ease, no shrinking from ridicule, contumely, or hatred, could turn him from the task imposed upon him, with awful sanctions, by the lips of the Eternal God."[1]

Or take the noble women with whose lofty virtue the inspired writers fill the sacred volumes, and whose names some of the books bear.

There is the sacred Book of *Ruth,* she who is called "friend" or "lover" in the Hebrew tongue, fair image of filial affection as she walks beside the aged Noemi along the weary roads north from Moab, to conduct her

---
[1] Geikie, "Hours With the Bible," v. 134.

mother to her native land. There, at noon and eve, we see her scan the fresh-mown fields for the gleanings which the law of Moses allowed the poor, in order that she might honorably keep the humble home of her widowed parent. Another sacred book we have which bears the name of *Judith*, the woman who, strengthened in the loyal love of her father's nation, by valiant deed set herself to defend the children of Israel from ignominious captivity. In the Book of *Esther* we have the history of her whose name signifies " myrtle," symbol among the Jews of joyous gratitude. Full of that modest wisdom of which Ecclesiasticus tells us that it " walketh with chosen women " (i. 17), her influence is typical of that which the Virgin Queen, fair Mother of the Christ, in later day did exercise upon the children of Eve. Ah, truly, " the word of God on high is the fountain of wisdom, and her ways are everlasting commandments " (Ecclesiastic.).

But it would be a lengthy task to point out all the details of manifold utility in the intellectual and practical, as well as the moral order, which come from the study of the Sacred Scripture. We have seen in a limited measure what it does for history, for language, for the science of government, for the development of general knowledge, and the cultivation of a graceful and vigorous style in writing. These books hold the key to true wisdom. " All Scripture," writes St. Paul to the young bishop Timothy, whom he himself had taught from the day he took him to himself as a boy at Lystra, "all Scripture, inspired by God, is profitable to teach, to reprove, to correct, to instruct."

Yet there are those, the same Apostle says, "who, always learning, never attain to the knowledge of truth" (II. Tim. iii. 7). Why? Because they do not study rightly.

XIV.

PROSPECTING.

"Man is the perfection of creation, the mind is the perfection of man, the heart is the perfection of the mind," says St. Francis de Sales.

Our aim is to become perfect in mind and heart, in character and disposition. Books are the readiest means of study to this end. They are at our command at all times. When we have discovered a beautiful thought, a strong chain of reasoning, which, whilst convincing, attracts and leads us into the domain of truth, however partial, we ponder it and make it our own, and we feel stronger in the permanent possession of it. We desire truth, and we look for it in books, mostly. Yet we may be anxious for knowledge, and worry or dream out our days in a course of reading without gaining any real advantage from it. Perhaps we fail in the proper choice of books, or else we do not observe the right method in reading and study.

Yet it is impossible for most men to go in search of and test everything that is labelled "*truth.*" Is there no remedy provided against the danger of oft going wrong in order to find the right? Yes. God has given us a compendium of everything that fosters true knowledge and wisdom in a book consigned to the direction of an old, experienced, and wise teacher. That book is the Bible, and the teacher is the Church of Christ. In the book we find a store of great truths, of all that is beautiful and ennobling, an infallible manual in the school of human perfection, which leads us so high that, having mastered its contents, we touch the very gates of heaven, where we may commune with the Creator of wisdom and of all that our souls are capable of knowing.

There are many who are thoroughly convinced of this. They believe that the Bible is the most perfect book on earth, that it is the book of books, as it has been called from time immemorial; for the word *Bible* means simply a book, *the* book of all others by excellence, as if there were none so worthy of study, and none which could not be dispensed with rather than this. And so it is. It contains all knowledge worthy of the highest aspirations and of the exercise of the best talents.

Yet, as a traveller in search of fortune may pass over seemingly barren tracts of desert land or mountain ridge, which treasure beneath the surface richest mines of gold, and caverns of splendid crystal and rarest marble, so the reader of the sacred books, in search of knowledge, may wearily tread along the paths of Bible truths, his eye bewildered by endless repetitions of precepts and monotonous scenes and seemingly uninteresting facts, unconscious of what wealth and beauty lie beneath him. And the reason of this listless and tiring sense in scanning over the pages of this book, which has from the first captivated the admiration of the noblest minds of every race and age, is the lack of sufficient preparation. The traveller looks for mines of gold and diamonds, but he has never learnt the art of prospecting. He stumbles over the heavy, dark ore, and the clods of metallic sand, and his feet toil along the path lined with pebbles that, if polished, would rival the stars of heaven, but they are a hindrance to him, for he does not know *that* or *how* he should examine and utilize their precious contents. He requires the previous training of the prospector, the sharp eye of the skilled mining master, and the unwearied courage to go down to examine the often crude-looking stones. Without these qualities he not only fails in his attainment of wealth, but becomes discouraged and even sceptic of its existence.

In other words, there are certain essential conditions required upon which depends the acquisition of that excellent knowledge which the Scriptures contain for every sphere of life. They are conditions which affect us in our entirety as men—I should say as the images of God, in whose likeness we were created. Sin has tarnished this image, and we are to restore it to its original beauty by correcting it. Our model is God Himself. The Bible is the text-book containing the image of this Model, drawn by Himself, and He has provided the preceptor to explain the various meanings of lines, lights, and shadows, and the use of the instruments which must be employed in completing the process. It is a little tedious, as all art training is in its beginning. Sometimes we copy with tracing-paper, and of late the kodak has done much to help us by the aid of photography.

XV.

USING THE KODAK.

You know that through the art of photography a perfect picture of an object may be produced by the action of light upon a smooth and sensitive surface. The light reflected from the object which is to be photographed enters through a lens into the dark chamber of the camera, and makes an impression upon the plate which is rendered sensitive by a film of chloride (or nitrate) of silver. To produce a good picture, therefore, three things are principally required:

1. *A faultless sensitized plate* on which the reflection of the object is to be made;

2. *A concentrated light;* that is, the rays must enter the camera through a lens, but be excluded from every other part;

3. *The right focus;* that is to say, you must get the proper distance of your object in order to preserve the just proportions between it and its surroundings.

The same requisites may be applied to ourselves when we wish to image in our souls the object of divine truth, which is identical with God.

1. The sensitive plate of our hearts and minds must be clean, without flaw, so as to admit the ray of heavenly light, and let it take hold upon its surface. A tarnished mirror gives but a blurred and imperfect reflection. Just so the mind occupied with the follies and vanities of worldliness, the heart filled with the changing idols of unworthy attachments, is no fit surface for the delicate impressions of those chaste delineations of truth which are nothing else but the image of God in the human soul. To His likeness we were created, and to His likeness we must again conform ourselves by a right study of truth.

2. Next, in order to obtain a correct impression of the sublime truth contained in the sacred volumes, we must concentrate our lights. That is to say, we must read with assiduity, must study with earnestness, and also with prayer, to obtain the light of the Divine Spirit who caused these pages of the Bible to be traced for our instruction—for, as one of our greatest English writers, though not a Catholic, has beautifully said:

"Within that awful volume lies
The mystery of mysteries!

Happiest they of human race
To whom God has granted grace
To read, to fear, to hope, to pray,
To lift the latch and force the way;
And better had they ne'er been born,
Who read to doubt, or read to scorn."[1]

This implies that all side-lights which may distract the mind from this concentrated attention and reverend attitude should be excluded. To read the Sacred Scriptures in a flippant mood, or even in an irreverent posture, and without having previously reflected on the fact that it is God's word, is to lessen immeasurably one's chance of profiting by the reading. The Mahometan or Jew in the East reverently lifts each piece of paper or parchment which he finds upon the road, for fear that it might contain the name of Allah or Jehovah, and be profaned by being trodden under foot. We owe no less to the inspired word of God, above all if we would gain the key to its intelligence.

The concentration into a focus is obtained through a perfectly-shaped, convex lens. Now this lens, which is capable not only of bringing into one strong point all the scattered rays of light, but under circumstances gathers the particles to intensity of heat producing a flame, is that centre of the affections commonly termed the heart. There is a tendency among those who seek intellectual culture to undervalue this quality of the heart,

---

[1] Scott, *The Monastery*, c. xii.

which nevertheless contains the secret power of generating supreme wisdom. We are considering true wisdom, not superficial, exclusively human wisdom, which is the very opposite, and which debases man to a mere repository of facts and impressions, like an illustrated encyclopedia, or makes of him a shrewd egotist, whose cleverness we may admire as we admire the antics of a dancing serpent without wishing to come in contact with its slimy body or its poisonous fangs.

"As in human things," says Pascal, " we must first know an object before we can love it, so in divine things, which constitute the only real truth at which man can worthily aim, we must love them before we can know them, for we cannot attain to truth except through charity." "In all our studies and pursuits of knowledge," says Watts, "let us remember that the conformation of our hearts to true religion and morality are things of far more consequence than all the furniture of our understanding and the richest treasures of mere speculative knowledge."

If it be true that "nothing is so powerful to form truly grand characters as meditation on the word of God and on Christian truths," then we must suppose an inclination, a love for the lofty ideals which Christianity sets before us. "To whom has the root of wisdom been revealed?" asks that wise and noble old rabbi, son of Sirach; and he answers: "God has given her to them that love Him." If the wise man in the sacred book tells us that "wisdom walketh with chosen women," may we not assume that it is because woman enjoys the prerogative of those qualities of heart which make her counsels so often far surer than the carefully pondered reasons of men?

If the fear of the Lord is the *beginning* of wisdom, is not charity or love its consummation? "Blessed is the man that shall continue in wisdom. With the bread of life and understanding God's fear shall feed him, and give him the water of wholesome wisdom to drink, and ... shall heap upon him a treasure of joy and gladness, and shall cause him to inherit an everlasting name. But ... foolish men shall not see her: for she is far from pride and deceit. ... Say not: It is through God that she is not with me, for do not thou the things that He hateth" (Eccles., ch. xiv. and xv.).

But there is no need of multiplying these sayings of God. The knowledge we seek here is the knowledge which comes from the Divine Spirit, source of all science as of all goodness and beauty. What the fruits of that spirit are we are told by St. Paul: Charity, joy, peace, patience, etc.; and we know how the Apostle of the Gentiles, who had learnt much in many schools, at the feet of Gamaliel and in the halls of the Greek philosophers, valued these fruits of wisdom above all the doctrines of men.

Catholics are fortunate in this, that they may gain from the study of the Bible that purest light of wisdom which is only partially communicated to those who find no way, through the sacraments, of cleansing their souls,—that mirror in which God's image can show clearly only when it is polished and purified from the dust-stains of our earthly fall. Whatever opportunities for thorough study of the Bible we may have, there can be no doubt that this is one of the most important conditions for its proper and fruitful appreciation, because the intelligence is always warped by sin.

A correct knowledge of our faith, as the primary rule of our conduct, is, of course, supposed. We cannot understand the written word of God unless we have become accustomed to the language He speaks to the heart, and that language is taught in our catechisms and text-books of religion. Some need less of this knowledge than others, so far as the difficulties and controversies of religion are concerned. The Bible is a book of instruction for all, and hence the preparatory knowledge required varies with the mental range and ability, and the consequent danger of doubts and false views of each individual. A child knows the precepts and wishes of its parent often by a look or gesture, without receiving any explicit instruction, because love and the habit of faith supply intelligence. Others require a certain amount of reasoning to move their hearts to the ready acceptance of divine precepts. This reasoning is supplied by the study of popular theologies, of which we have a good number in English.

3. Lastly, we must not only get a right glass, a good lens, but we must likewise get the right focus for our picture. We must know the distance of our objects and their surroundings, the lights and shades, the coloring, natural and artificial. In other words, we must become familiar with the circumstances of history, the dates, the places, the customs and laws, national and social, which throw light upon the meaning of the incidents related in the Sacred Scriptures, and which often aid us in the interpretation of passages mysterious and prophetic. Hence we have to give some attention to, and study what we can, of the ancient records and monuments brought to light by the archæologist and the historian. We must likewise inquire into the origin, history, authority, purpose, and general argument of each of the inspired books. All this is the object of what is called *Introduction to the Study of the Sacred Scriptures*, and is nothing else but a becoming and essential preparation for the right use of the Bible.

> Ah, may our understanding ever read
> This glorious volume which God's wisdom made,
> And in that charter humbly recognize
> Our title to a treasure in the skies!

XVI.

THE INTERPRETATION OF THE IMAGE.

The Bible is not only a text-book which leads us to the acquisition of the highest of arts—that of fulfilling the true purpose of life—but it is itself, as has already been suggested, a work of fairest art inasmuch as it contains a perfect delineation of the divine Beauty drawn by the sovereign Artist Himself.

Now true art needs, as a rule, an interpretation; for the outward form which appeals to the senses may have its deeper and real meaning disguised beneath the figure, so as to be understood only by the finer perceptions of the intellect and heart. Take, for example, a canvas such as Millet's popular picture entitled "The Angelus." It is a small, unpretentious-looking work, representing a youth and a maid in a fallow field, a village church in the distance, all wrapt in the gloom of eventide. Ask a child looking at the picture what is the meaning of it, and it will probably answer: "Two poor people tired of work." Ask a countryman, without much education, and he will say: "Two poor lovers thinking of home." But to the poet who has perchance dwelt in some village of fair Southern France, and knows the simple habits of devotion among the peasant folk, the picture will awaken memories of the sound of the Angelus:

> "Ave Maria," blessed be the hour,
> The time, the clime, the spot where I so oft
> Have felt that moment in its fullest power
> Sink o'er the earth, so beautiful and soft,
> While swung the deep bell in the distant tower,
> Or the faint dying day-hymn stole aloft,
> And not a breath crept through the rosy air.

And the reflecting, devout Catholic will see in that picture even more than the thoughts it suggests to the poet. It will speak to him of the angelic salute to a Virgin fair at Nazareth; it will touch a chord of tender confidence and hope in the Madonna's help and sympathy; it will arouse a feeling of gratitude for the mystery of the Redemption. And all this difference of judgment arises from the varying degrees of intelligence and knowledge with which we approach the image.

Now the Sacred Scriptures present just such a picture, only larger, more comprehensive, truer, deeper, containing all the fair delineation of God's own image, the pattern according to which we are to correct the same divine likeness in our souls, spoiled somewhat and blurred by sin.

Let us look at the outline. There are words and a fact. In the words truth is enunciated, in the fact those words are exhibited as being a divine utterance. In their *literal* meaning the word affects us just as a picture would at first sight. In the one case we have a precept or an incident or a scene in the life of our Lord; in the other case we have an act of prayer or a scene from the daily life of French peasants. But just as in the picture we may, by reason of artistic and spiritual culture, recognize not simply an ordinary scene of peasant life, but a poetic thought, or a practical moral lesson calling for imitation, or, finally, a mystery of religion, so in the Sacred Scriptures we may see below the literal sense one that is internal, hidden, and in its character either simply figurative, or moral, or mystically spiritual. An old ecclesiastical writer has given us a Latin hexameter which suggests these various senses in which the sacred text may at times be understood:

> Litera *gesta* docet, quod credas *allegoria;*
> *Moralis* quid agas, quo tendas *anagogia.*

An example of the four different senses (namely, the *literal,* the *allegorical,* which appeals to our faith, the *moral,* and the *mystic*) in which a word or passage of Holy Writ may be interpreted is offered in the term "Jerusalem." If we read that "they went up to Jerusalem every year," we understand the word Jerusalem to represent the chief city of the Hebrews, situated on the confines of Judah and Benjamin. If we happen upon the passage of St. John where he says: "I, John, saw a holy city, the new Jerusalem, coming down out of heaven from God; ... behold the tabernacle of God with men, and He will dwell with them," we know that this *new* Jerusalem on earth can be no other than the Church, where God has His tabernacle, dwelling with men. The word is used *allegorically,* that is to say, it appeals to our faith; to the internal, not to our external sense. Again, the word "Jerusalem" may be used in the sense which its etymology suggests without reference to any city. Etymologically it consists of two words, signifying *foundation* and *peace.* A rabbi might, therefore, bid his disciples to strive to build up "Jerusalem," meaning that they should seek to lay solid foundations of peace by conforming their lives to the law of Jehovah. This would give the word Jerusalem simply a *moral* signification. Finally, the word is used as a synonyme for "heaven," as in Apoc. xxi. 10: "And He took me up in spirit, . . . and He showed me the holy city Jerusalem, . . . having the glory of God." Here we have the term in its *anagogical* sense, that is, referring to the future life.

Without entering into the various figures of speech with which the language of the Hebrews abounds, let me suggest some points which must be observed in order that the true sense of the Sacred Scriptures may not escape us so as to mislead the mind.

For the discovery of the literal sense we must, of course, be guided by the rules of ordinary grammatical construction. Where this proves insufficient we must have recourse to the idiomatic use of language, the habits of speech, which prevailed among the Hebrews or those with whose utterances or history we are concerned. This is very important in order that we may get a right understanding of the expressions employed. As an instance of misconception in this respect may be cited the words of our Lord to His holy Mother at the nuptials of Cana, which literally sound like a reproof, yet are far from conveying such a sense in their original signification. The like is true of the use of certain comparisons which to our sense seem rude and cruel, yet which were not so understood in the language in which they were originally spoken or written. Thus when our Lord said to the Canaanitish woman who followed Him in the regions of Tyre and Sidon that it is not right to give the bread of the children to "dogs," He seemed to spurn the poor mother, who prayed Him for the recovery of her child, as a man spurns a cur. Yet such is not the sense of the expression, which hardly means anything more than what we would convey by "outside of the pale of faith."

Besides the usage of speech peculiar to a people or district or period of time, we must have regard to the individuality of the writer. His subjective state, his temperament, education, personal associations, and habits of thought and feeling necessarily influence the style of his writing. Thus in the letters of St. Paul we recognize a spirit which the forms of speech seem wholly inadequate to contain or express. He writes as he might speak, impatient of words. His thoughts seem often disconnected; he omits things which he had evidently meant to say, and which the hearers might have supplied from the vividness of the image presented, but which become obscure to the reader who only sees the cold form of the written page. There is no end of parenthetical clauses in his discourses; often he begins a period and leaves it unfinished. Sometimes there appears a total absence of logical connection in what he intends for proofs and arguments; then, again, there is a wealth of imagery, which suggests the quick sense and power of comparison peculiar to the Oriental mind, but slow to impress itself on the Western nations. All this makes it necessary to *study* St. Paul rather than to read him, if one would understand the Apostle. Of this St. Peter shows himself conscious when he writes that certain things in the Epistles of St. Paul are "*hard to be understood*, which the unlearned and unstable wrest, as they do also the other Scriptures, to their own destruction" (II. Pet. iii. 16).

Another element which contributes to the right interpretation of the Sacred Text is the knowledge of what may be called the historical background of a passage or book. This includes the various relations of time, place, persons addressed, and other circumstances which exercise an influence upon the material, intellectual, and moral surroundings of the writer. Accordingly, different parts of the Sacred Scriptures require different treatment and different preparation on the part of the reader. Thus to comprehend the full significance of the Book of Exodus we must study the geographical and ethnographical condition of Egypt. For a right understanding of the Book of Daniel we should first have to become acquainted with the history of Chaldea and Assyria, especially as lit up by the recent discoveries of monuments in the East. The Canticle of Canticles presupposes for its just interpretation a certain familiarity with the details of Solomon's life during the golden period of his reign. The Letters of St. Paul, in the New Testament, reveal their true bearing only after we have read the life of the Apostle as it is described in the Acts; and so on for other parts of the Sacred History.

Finally, a proper understanding and appreciation of the inspired books depend largely on our realization of the proximate scope and purpose, the character and quality, of the subject treated by the sacred writer. The Bible is a wondrous combination of historic, didactic, and prophetic elements. Each of these goes to support or emphasize the other, but each of them has its predominant functions in different parts of the grand structure. Hence we may not judge a prophecy as we judge the historical narrative which introduces and supports it; we may not interpret in its literal sense the metaphor which is simply to convey a moral lesson to the mind.

XVII.

"DEUS ILLUMINATIO MEA."

The subject-matter of the Bible obliges us, however, to apply not only the various cautions and methods of interpretation which are required for the understanding of the classics generally, but it exacts more. The Sacred Scriptures, as a grand work of art, have not only a human, but primarily a divine conception for their basis. Hence it does not suffice to have mastered the meaning of the words and the outline of the subject, or the individual genius and human ideal of the writer who acted merely as the instrument executing a higher inspiration. We must enter into the conception of the divine mind. If the principal and all-pervading motive of the great Scriptural composition is a religious one, it stands to reason that it can be comprehended only when judged from a religious point of view.

Now the divine mind is so far above us that we can reach it only if God Himself brings it down to us. He has to descend, to lift the veil from His immensity, not by opening to us, before the time, those sacred precincts which "eye hath never seen," but by emitting a ray of light to clear up our darkness, to give us a glimpse of the awful splendor which vibrates in those celestial realms where light and sound and warmth of eternal charity mingle in the sweet harmony of the divine Beauty whose tones speak now to our senses in separate forms. God descends to our humility to interpret His own image. First He came in human form, and told us all the things we were to believe and do. Then He sent the Paraclete, and under His direction men of God taught the same things. Then they wrote them, or, as St. John tells us, some of them. The Paraclete veils Himself, as our Lord had announced to His Apostles, in the Church, whose divinely constituted earthly chief was to be Peter—to the end of time. The Church, therefore, founded by Christ, and an ever-living emanation of the incessant activity of the Holy Spirit, although necessarily speaking to men through men, is the first and surest interpreter of the purpose and meaning of each and every part of Holy Writ.

And because God cannot contradict Himself it follows that every truth of the written word must correspond with every truth of the spoken word. In doubtful cases, therefore, as to the meaning of a word or text in the Sacred Writings, we have recourse to the supreme, divinely-guided judgment of the Church. Her doctrines, defined, are the first and most important criterion of Scriptural truth.

But the Church has not defined every expression of truth, though she holds the key to all truth. She points to the light which illumines our night; she declares the stars whence that light issues directly or by reflection;

but she does not always indicate where the rays of the one body begin to mingle with those of the other, or what precise elements determine the motion or stability of each. Only when there are conflicts or threatened disturbances of the centres of attraction and repulsion she reaches out her anointed hand, informed with the magic power of her Creator and founder, and directs the courses of bodies that otherwise would clash unto mutual destruction. Hence the freedom of investigation allowed the Catholic student of the Scriptures is limited only by the rules of faith taught by the same divine Teacher who watches over the spoken and written revelation alike. And as, in cases where we have not the express command of a superior, we interpret his will by his known desires and views in other respects, so in the interpretation of those parts of Holy Writ regarding the meaning of which we have no definite expression in the doctrinal code of the Church, we follow the *analogy of faith;* which is manifest from the general consent of the Christian Fathers and Doctors, and from the teaching of learned and holy commentators. These we may safely follow in all doubtful cases, that is to say, where there is no evidence to show that they were mistaken, either through want of certain sources of information or proofs which we have at our command presently, or because they accepted the views of their time and people, feeling that any departure from the received tradition would make disturbance, and fail of its intended good effect.

It is safe to say that the conditions of one age and the modes of thought and feeling of one generation are not a just standard by which to judge the conditions and views of another age or generation. This is an important fact to remember for those who are inclined to look in every part of the Sacred Scriptures for a verification of the sentiments which they feel, and of the views and opinions of things which they hold.

XVIII.

RUSH-LIGHTS.

There is a method of interpreting the Bible which, although it affords a temporary satisfaction to the heart, is misleading to the mind. I mean private interpretation in the sense in which it is generally practised and defended by our Protestant brethren. To take a good photograph you must have sunlight; candles, gas, even electric lights, unless they be flash-lights, which don't suit all purposes of accurate reproduction, will not accomplish it. For vegetable growth you need sunlight; artificial light will give neither healthy fruit nor even color to the plant. So it is with the divine image traced in the Sacred Scriptures. We cannot reproduce it in our souls by any earthly light. Now human judgment is an earthly light, because it is constantly influenced by feelings, prejudices, attachments, and partial views of things. Some of us accept an opinion because it suits our conditions of life, is agreeable to our sense of ease or vanity, relieves us from certain responsibilities to God and our neighbor which a severer statement of the case would exact. Others endorse a view because it is held by a person whom they love or respect. Others, again, maintain an opinion because it is contrary to the one held by a person whom they dislike. And there is a vast number of people who take a view simply because it is the first that presents itself to them, and they are as well pleased with it as with others which they don't know. It must be remembered, moreover, that man is not naturally inclined toward the right. The world loves darkness since its eyes were hurt by the wanton effort to see God and to be like Him in a way which was against His law. Amid this darkness, intellectual and moral, which surrounds man, and which for the moment pleases him because it relieves him of a strain, we need a guide. We must follow a leader who knows all the ways and enjoys the full light of heaven.

The defence in favor of private interpretation of the Bible usually rests in the assumption of God's goodness, who must needs furnish an inward light to man lest he go wrong in his search after truth. But God's goodness gives you a guide, well accredited with testimonials from Himself, against whose efficiency the inward light compares like a rush-light against the sun.

The red cross of the Alpine Club marks the safe passage down the rocky mountain paths of Switzerland. We recognize the stones which are landmarks because they bear the conventional sign of an authorized body of mountaineers. They lead our way, and we follow without hesitation. But if the mark of the red cross of the Alpine Club were not visible, if we had to trust to the inward light or to our instinct to guide us, we should run the risk of losing our way and lives, though the stones which marked the path of former travellers are still there.

Nor does it seem according to the divine wisdom to give man a written law and then to leave him to Himself for its interpretation. No other written law was ever given under such conditions by or to man. It would frustrate the fundamental purpose of any written law to allow the individual to interpret it, because it would lead to contradictions and confusion, which it is the very object of laws to prevent. That the divine Law, in its written form, is no exception to this rule is proved from the effects of the theory of private interpretation, which have grown into a history of many sects, conscientiously protesting one against the other because of the inferences which each draws from the one sacred code of Christian law and doctrine. Thus the written word of God would frustrate its own manifest purpose, nay, give occasion to a thousand justifications of separation and hostility, which its fundamental canon, charity in the union of Christ, expressly forbids.

What other conclusion, therefore, remains than to accept the warning of St. Peter, Prince of the Apostles, who, speaking of the reading of the Sacred Scriptures, wishes the converts to understand *" this, first, that no prophecy of Scripture is made by private interpretation,"* [1] because *" the holy men of God spoke, inspired by the Holy Ghost "* (II. Pet. i. 20, 21).

And this disposes, in the mind of the sincere Christian, of all the theories of interpretation advanced by rationalist and naturalist philosophers, who render their arguments a trifle more consistent than Protestants by denying from the outset the divine inspiration of the Sacred Scriptures.

[1] The Protestant (King James) version of this passage reads : " That no prophecy of the Scripture is of any private interpretation." The late revision of the New Testament omits the word *any.*

XIX.

THE USE AND THE ABUSE OF THE BIBLE.

"Revelation and a Church are practically identical. Revelation and Scripture are not."[1] Though *revelation* is necessary to guide the human mind, prone to error, and to sustain the human will, weak by reason of an hereditary fall, we have seen that the Bible is but *one* channel of that revelation, and that a complementary, secondary one. It neither contains all revealed truth, nor can the truth which it contains be clearly and completely understood without the guidance of an intelligent interpretation. A teacher of any science or art may give a book into the hands of his pupils to serve as a text, as a reminder of his precepts, as a compend of his methods and practice; but no book, no matter how perfectly written, will make us dispense with the teacher. The education, in any direction, which rests upon the sole use of books is essentially defective and misleading.

This is eminently true of the Bible as a text or guide in the acquisition of the highest of arts, the profoundest of sciences, which leads us to the recognition of absolute truth, with an ever-increasing apprehension, because its scope is immeasurable, eternal.

The teacher of revelation, in its first and most impor-

[1] Humphrey, "The Sacred Scriptures," *l. c.*

tant signification, is Christ. He is the central historical figure, announced to man immediately after his fall in Paradise foreshadowed by the prophets in the Jewish Church, and completing His mission in the Christian Church. As the Holy Ghost animated the prophets to foretell Him, and the priests of the synagogue to announce Him in the Old Law, so the Holy Ghost animates the Church to continue His work in the New Law. As books were written by the prophets of old to perpetuate the remembrance of what Jehovah had spoken through them to His people regarding the coming of the Messias, so books were written by the Apostles and disciples of the New Law to perpetuate the remembrance of what that Messias had said and done, and of what He wished us to do. But as the old written Law was not to be a substitute for the commission of teaching and guiding the people through the Jewish Synagogue, so neither was the new written Law intended to be a substitute for the commission of teaching and guiding those who seek salvation through Christ. The Bible alone, as we have already seen, cannot satisfy us in such a way as to supply the full reason for our faith in Christ's teaching. For this we have a Church to whom Christ, as God, gave a direct commission, without adding a book, or an express command to write a book.

But a book was written, written under the guidance of the divine Spirit, who had been promised to the Church whenever it would speak, whether by word of mouth or by epistle and written gospel. And that book, though not containing all truth, contains truth only. Therefore it is useful, as St. Paul says, II. Tim. iii. 16: "All Scripture inspired of God is profitable to teach, to reprove, to correct, to instruct in justice, that the man of God may be perfect, furnished to every good work." The *use*, then, of the Bible is to teach, to instruct in justice, primarily; to make man perfect, furnished to every good work. Mark the twofold term: to *teach* and to *instruct;* both teaching and instruction to serve the one end—to make a perfect man, "furnished to every good work."

That the principal purpose and scope of Scripture is to teach the truths of religion has been demonstrated in a former chapter. I have here only to add that, as an instrument of Apologetics, and in discussion with Protestants who admit the divinity of Christ and the inspired character of the Sacred Scriptures, reference to the teachings of the Bible plays a very important part. Whether we are defending our faith against misrepresentation, or desirous of convincing other sincere and open minds of the justness of the claims which the Catholic Church makes as the only true representative of Christ's divine mission to teach the nations, the Bible is a safe and commonly recognized meeting-ground for a fair discussion of the subject.

Even when we have to speak of religion with practical infidels, who read the Bible, or have some knowledge of its contents, that book will serve us as a powerful weapon of defence and persuasion. Few intelligent men or women of to-day, especially if they are earnest, and have a real regard for virtue and truth, though they may consider them as mere gifts of the natural order, fail to recognize that Christianity is a power for good, and that Christ, its Author, is and ever will be the great teacher of mankind, in whose true following man becomes better, nobler, and happier. To illustrate this fact, we may be permitted to quote at some length from an article by Baron Von Hügel in a recent number of the *Dublin Review* (April, 1895). Speaking of Christ, he cites from various writers, as follows:

Thus "Ernest Rénan, sceptical even to his own scepticism, addresses him and says: 'A thousand times more living, a thousand times more loved, since thy death than during thy passage upon earth, thou wilt become the corner-stone of humanity, to such a point, that to blot out thy name out of the world would be in very truth to shake its very foundations.'[1] John Stuart Mill, who tells us of himself: 'I never lost faith, for I never had it,' proclaims at the end of his long life's labors: 'Whatever else may be taken from us by rational criticism, Christ is still left; a unique figure, not more unlike all his predecessors than all his followers, even those who had the direct benefit of his personal teaching. It is no use to say that Christ in the Gospels is not historical, and that we know not how much of what is admirable has been superadded by the tradition of his followers. For who among his disciples or their

[1] " Vie de Jésus," 1864, p. 426.

proselytes was capable of inventing the sayings ascribed to
Jesus, or of imagining the life and character revealed in the
Gospels? Certainly not the fishermen of Galilee, as certainly
not St. Paul, whose character and idiosyncrasy were of a total-
ly different sort; still less the early Christian writers, in whom
nothing is more evident than that the good which was in them
was all derived, as they always professed that it was derived,
from the higher source.'[1] Even so purely Deistic a critic as
Abraham Kuenen declares: 'The international religion which
we call Christianity was founded, not by the Apostle Paul, but
by Jesus of Nazareth, that Jesus whose person and whose teaching are sketched in the Synoptic Gospels with the closest ap-
proximation of truth.' 'The need of Christianity is as keen as
ever. It is not for less but for more Christianity that the age
cries out. Even those many who do not identify Christianity
with the ecclesiastical form in which they themselves profess it,
and who have no confidence that the world will necessarily conform to them—even these may be at peace. The universalism
of Christianity is the sheet-anchor of their hope. A history of
eighteen centuries bears mighty witness to it; and the contents
of its evidence and the high significance they possess are brought
into the clearest light by the comparison with other religions.
We have good courage then.'[2] So advanced a critic and sensi-
tively loyal a Jew as Mr. Claud Montefiore tells us: 'Some of the
sayings ascribed to Jesus have sunk too deep into the human
heart, or shall I say into the spiritual consciousness of civilized
mankind, to make it probable that any religion which ignores
or omits them will exercise a considerable influence outside its
own borders. It may be that those who dream of a prophetic

[1] " Three Essays on Religion," 1874, p. 258.
[2] " Hibbert Lectures," 1882, pp. 196, 197.

The Use and Abuse of the Bible. 101

Judaism, which shall be as spiritual as the religion of Jesus, and even more universal than the religion of Paul, are the victims of a delusion.'[1] So largely naturalistic a critic as Julius Wellhausen writes of our Lord's teaching and person: 'The miraculous is impossible with man, but with God it is possible. Jesus has not only assured us of this, but he has proved it in his own person. He had indeed lost his life and saved it, he could do as he would. He had escaped the bonds of human kind and the sufferings of self-seeking nature. There is in him no trace of that eagerness for action which seeks for peace in the restlessness of its own activity. The completely super-worldly standpoint in which Jesus finds strength and love to devote himself to the world has nothing extravagant about it. He is the first to know himself, not simply in moments of emotion, but in completest restfulness, the child of God; before him no one so felt or so described himself.' 'Jesus not only prophesies the kingdom of God, but brings it out of its transcendence on to earth; he plants at least its germ. The new times already begin with him: the blind see, the deaf hear, the dead arise. Everywhere he found spaciousness for his soul, nowhere was he cramped by the little, much as he put forward the value of the great; this we should do, and not leave that undone. He was more than a prophet; in him the word had become flesh. The historic overweightedness, to which the Jews were succumbing, does not even touch him. A unit arises in the dreary mass, a man from among the rubbish which the dwarfs, the rabbis, had heaped up. He upsets the accidental, the caricature, the dead, and collects the eternally valid, the human divine, in the focus of His individuality. "Ecce homo," a divine wonder in this time and this environment.'"

[1] Ibid., 1892, p. 551.

Such being the view of religiously disposed persons outside of the Catholic Church regarding the New Testament teaching of Christ, it would seem easy at first sight to convince them of the Catholic doctrine by reference to the words of Christ and the Gospels, which contain explicit, if not complete testimony in behalf of the Catholic teaching. There is one difficulty in the way of this, and that is that Protestants themselves distrust the meaning of the New Testament words except in so far as it expresses their own feelings. The principle of private interpretation necessarily leads to this one-sided view. A hundred persons appeal to the one Book as an infallible expression of God's will and truth. Now, some of these infallible expressions manifestly contradict one another as Protestants interpret them. Yet the consequences of such contradictions are vital, and involve eternal life or death. Take the doctrine of baptism by water as essential to salvation, according to the reading of some Protestants; yet the Quaker, no less sincere than his Baptist neighbor, and claiming a special inward light, consciously neglects baptism, holding that the teaching of the New Testament is only meant in a spiritual sense. Equally awful in their consequences are the two contrary doctrines regarding the Eucharistic presence of Christ as declared in the New Testament, one believer drawing the conclusion that he must adore God under the veil of bread, the other equally convinced from the same Scriptures that such a view is sheer idolatry, and that there is nothing divine under the appearance of bread. This appeal to private judgment makes most Protestants sceptical if you attempt to prove to them Catholic doctrine from the New Testament; and unless you can first convince them that the Church has a greater claim to declare the sense of the Bible than any private individual, they will consider their opinion of its meaning and purpose just as good as yours.

But it is different if you appeal to the Old Testament for a confirmation of Catholic doctrine. And I would strongly urge this method for various reasons. Every Protestant will admit that the Old Testament is not only inspired and divine in its origin, but that in its historic expression, even the deutero-canonical portion, contains the application of its meaning and purpose. In other words, that God not merely gave the Israelites a law, but also shows us how He meant them to interpret that law in their lives—domestic, social, and religious. Here, therefore, we have little need, or even opportunity, for private interpretation as to God's meaning. That meaning becomes clear from the action of His people.

At the same time it is also clear and generally admitted that the Old Testament is a foreshadowing of the New Law, hence that the doctrines and practices of the Christian Church have their counterpart in the Old Law. Protestants readily agree to this, in proof of which fact I may be allowed to quote Prof. Robertson Smith:

"Christianity can never separate itself from its historical basis, or the religion of Israel; the revelation of God in Christ cannot be divorced from the earlier revelation on which our Lord built. Indeed, the history of Israel, when rightly studied, is the most real and vivid of all histories; and the proofs of God's working among His people of old may still be made, what they were in time past, one of the strongest evidences of Christianity."[1]

Dr. A. B. Bruce in his *Apologetics*, 1892, p. 325, says: "The Bible, instead of being a dead rule, to be used mechanically, with equal value set on all its parts, is rather a living organism, which, like the butterfly, passes through various transformations before arriving at its highest and final form. We should find Christ in the Old Testament as we find the butterfly in the caterpillar."[2]

Hence if you can show to the average intelligent Protestant that a doctrine or practice distinctively of the Catholic Church prevailed in the Jewish Church, you have established an *a priori* argument for its reasonableness. This applies particularly to such doctrines and practices as Protestants condemn or censure in the Catholic Church from a mere habit of not finding them in their own churches, or from some prejudice nourished by bigotry of early teachers, or by the popular literature of the anti-Catholic type. I only mention such topics as In-

---

[1] "The Old Testament in the Jewish Church," 1892, p. 11.
[2] See *Dublin Review*, article cited above.

dulgences, Confession, the Infallibility of the Pope, Celibacy of the clergy and religious, and such like. Now all these things existed in the Old Law, not so completely developed as in the Christian Church, but sufficiently pronounced to establish a motive of credibility for their existence in the Church of Christ. Thus we have the reasonableness of the practice of Confession plainly indicated in the Mosaic times: "And the Lord spoke to Moses, saying: Say to the children of Israel, when a man or woman shall have committed any of all the sins that men are wont to commit, and by negligence shall have transgressed the commandment of the Lord, and offended, they shall confess their sin, and shall restore the principal itself, and the fifth part over and above, to him against whom they have sinned" (Num. v. 6-7; also 13-14). The Infallibility of the Pope finds its perfect counterpart in the oracular responses given by the Jewish high-priest when he wore the Urim and Thummim in his breastplate, which covers the precise ground of Papal decisions regarding faith and morals, the breastplate being called "the rational of judgment, doctrine, and truth" (See Exod. xxviii. 30; Levit. viii. 8; Num. xxvii. 21; Deut. xxxiii. 8, etc.).

As to the practice of virginity, we know that it existed among the Jews, as an exceptional condition; but as such it had the sanction of God. Thus the Prophet Jeremias receives the command of virginity from Jehovah directly: "And the word of the Lord came to me, saying: Thou shalt not take thee a wife; neither shalt thou have sons and daughters in this place" (Jer. xvi. 2).

Thus practical arguments, of which I can here only indicate a few, may be found for each and all of the usages of the Catholic Church. And any censure of the latter will cast its reflection upon the Jewish dispensation, of which God was Himself the Author and Guardian. For if God sanctioned ceremonies in worship, and infallibility in the high-priest, and virginity in the Prophet whom He selects for a special mission, and confession, with penance and the obligation of restitution, why should Protestants think it so strange to find us practise the same things which have the seal of divine approbation!

Thus they may be inclined more readily to accept the more explicit arguments in favor of Catholic doctrine and discipline as given in the New Testament, which is but the fulfilment of the types suggested in the Old Law.

It is hardly necessary for me to point out in this connection the advantages of being able to disabuse Protestants of the impression that Catholics do not honor the Bible as the word of God. Those who, as Protestants, do not recognize any other source of divine revelation than the written word are, of course, obliged to occupy themselves wholly and entirely with its study, whilst Catholics look upon that same written word, not

The Use and Abuse of the Bible. 107

with less reverence, but with less consciousness of having to rely upon it as the only symbol and exponent of their faith. If we refuse on general principles to have the Bible read to our Catholic children in a public school from a Protestant translation, it is simply because the admission of such a practice implies an admission of a Protestant principle, and might leave a wrong impression upon our children as to the value of the true version of their religion. The Protestant translation of the Bible contains a great deal of truth, *but some errors* which we cannot admit in our teaching. To give it to our children in the schools is something like planting a Southern flag upon some public institution of the United States. Some may say it is better than none, because it begets patriotism, and as there is no difference in the two flags except the slight one of a few stars and stripes, most people might never notice it. But we know that if they did notice it, it would create considerable disturbance, because it implies something of disloyalty to "Old Glory."

For a like reason Catholics often refuse to kiss the Protestant Bible in court. They prefer simply to *affirm*. And in this they are perfectly right, although to attest one's willingness to tell the truth on such occasions is not supposed to be a trial of one's faith, and hence it does not involve anything of a denial of Catholic truth.

But I must pass on to one or two illustrations to show in what fields the Bible is *not* to be used. For though it furnishes most apt means for imparting a knowledge and inciting to the further study of history, languages, the principles of government and ethics, together with the development of a graceful and withal vigorous style of English writing, yet there are limits to its use in some directions. Thus the Bible cannot be considered as replacing the exact sciences. We are quite safe always in affirming that the Bible never contradicts science; that where it does not incidentally confirm the results of scientific research it abstracts from the teaching of science. Its language relating to physical facts is popular, not scientific. There is no reason to think that the inspired writers received any communication from heaven as to the inward workings of nature. They had simply the knowledge of their age, and described things accordingly. Leo XIII. in his recent Encyclical on the study of the Sacred Scriptures strongly reiterates this doctrine, advanced by many Doctors of the Church, namely, that the *sacred writers* had no intention of initiating us into the secrets of nature or to teach us the inward constitution of the visible world. Hence their language about "the firmament," and how "the sun stood still," as we still say "the sun rises."[1]

If, then, we are confronted with some statement by

---

[1] See Humphrey, "The Sacred Scriptures;" also "*Questions Actuelles d'-Ecriture Sainte,*" by Brucker, S. J.

scientists affirming that there is a scientific inaccuracy in the Bible, we have no remark to make but that the Bible was not meant to be a text-book of exact science. If it is urged that there are contradictions between the Bible and science, then the case demands attention. We know that truth cannot contradict itself; but we know that we may err in apprehending it, and that science may err in its assumptions of fact. Hence in the matter of Biblical Apology, when dealing with science, it is of the first importance that we render an exact account to ourselves of what *science affirms* and of what the *Sacred Scripture affirms*. It is important to note here the distinction which P. Brucker points out; namely, what *science affirms, not* what *scientists affirm*. "The latter often mingle *conjecture*, more or less probable, with the definitely ascertained results of scientific experiment; they often accept as facts certain observations and plausible conclusions which are not always deduced from legitimate premises nor in a strictly logical method." The human mind is always prone to accept the plausible for the true, the appearance of things for their substance, the general for the universal, the part for the whole, or the probable for the proved. This is demonstrated by the history of scientific hypotheses in nearly every department of human knowledge.

In the next place, we must be quite sure to ascertain *what the Sacred Scriptures affirm*. Apologists place themselves in a needlessly responsible position when, in the difficult task of determining a doubtful reading of the Sacred Text, they assume an interpretation which may be gainsaid by scientific *proof.* The teaching of St. Augustine and St. Thomas on this subject is that we are not to interpret in any *particular* sense any part of Sacred Scripture which admits of a different interpretation. And here Leo XIII. in his Encyclical gives us an important point to consider when he says that the defenders of the Sacred Scriptures must not consider that they are obliged to defend *each single* opinion of isolated Fathers of the Church.[1] There is a difference between a *prudent conservatism* and a timid and slavish repetition of time-honored views. Also between *an intelligent advance* of well-founded, though *new* views, and an excessive temerity, which rashly replaces the tradition of ages by the suggestions of new science.

"Hence any attempt to prove that the statements of the Bible imply in every case exact conformity with the latest results of scientific research is a needless and, under circumstances, a dangerous experiment; for although there are instances where (as in chap. i. of Genesis) the Bible statements anticipate the exactest results of scientific investigation by many centuries, yet it is not and need not be so in all instances.

"Yet whilst we may not consider Moses as anticipating the investigations of a Newton, a Laplace, or a Cuvier, there are cases where the natural purpose and con-

[1] See Appendix.

text of the sacred writers develop an exact harmony with the facts of science of which former ages had no right conception. Such are the creation by successive stages, the unity of species, and origin of the human race, etc. But these facts are *not proposed as scientific revelations.*"

In all important questions as to the agreement of the Bible with the results of scientific research we may have recourse with perfect confidence to the living teaching of the Church; where she gives no decision there we are at liberty to speculate, provided the results of our speculation do not conflict with explicit and implied doctrines of truth, that is to say, they must be in harmony with the general analogy of faith.

There is one other topic which I would touch upon in speaking of the use and abuse of the Bible; it is a view which the late Oliver Wendell Holmes is supposed to have advocated. The author of " The Professor at the Breakfast Table " believed that it would be advantageous if the Bible were, as he terms it, *depolarized,* that is to say, if the translations or versions made from the originals were put in such form as to appeal to the imagination and feelings of the present generation by substituting modern terminology and figures of speech for the old time-honored words of Scriptural comparisons. The aim would be, as I understand it, to do for the written word of God what the Salvation Army leaders are attempting to do for nineteenth century Christianity in general.

In answer to this suggestion it may be said that the attempt has been made in various ways, and seemingly always without result for the better. As we have versions of St. Paul's Epistles in Ciceronian Latin, so we have had travesties of the Gospels intended to popularize the moral maxims they contain. If it is question of making the Bible accessible to the people for the purpose of getting them to read it, devices of this kind may succeed to a degree with those who look for novelty. As to its essential form, the Bible is popular,—appeals to all minds and conditions. This is proved by the experience of centuries, in every clime and among all races.

Those parts which do not directly appeal to a popular sentiment are of a nature to forbid depolarization as above suggested, since in changing them they would necessarily lose their identity, the inherent proofs of their origin, and their underlying mystic and spiritual meaning. So far as they were written, the truths contained in the Bible were to serve all time. To change their form is to tamper with the spirit of a divine language, which, although it comes to us in human sounds, variable according to nationality and time and place, still has an unction, a breath of heaven accompanying it which would vanish as the perfume vanishes from the transplanted flower. There are some truths, some ideas and feelings, which cannot be expressed in popular fashion without losing their essential qualities. One might urge the same reasons in behalf of painting the old Greek statues, because the common people would find it possible to admire them if gaudy coloring helped their imagination to interpret the action of the figures in marble. Some things in the Bible were not written for all, and appeal only to refined and spiritual minds. Others can be easily understood and assimilated, and there are preachers commissioned to make attractive and intelligible that which of itself does not appeal to the rude. There is such a thing as *accommodating* the words of the Sacred Scripture for the purpose of impressing a truth by analogy, and of the use of this method we have beautiful illustrations in the writings of the Fathers and in the Offices of the Breviary. But the sense *by accommodation,* as it is called by writers on hermeneutics, does not take liberties with the Sacred Text itself in the manner suggested by the advocates of *depolarization.* For the rest there is a difference, there always will be a difference, between the qualities that call upon the senses and attract, perhaps, the larger circle of admirers, and that choicer spirit which reaches the soul. You cannot substitute one for the other; their domain is widely apart, though they may use the same instrument.

> One tunes his facile lyre to please the ear,
> And win the buzzing plaudits of the town;
> The other sings his soul out to the stars,
> And the deep hearts of men.

You cannot depolarize, without destroying, Dante, or Milton, or any of our great poets; no more can you depolarize the great masterpiece of the Bible. Let us take it as we receive it under the guardianshp of the Church. Its apparent imperfections are like the surroundings and exterior of its Founder: a scandal to the Greek, a stumbling-block to the Jew, because they could not realize that a God was hidden in the imperfect guise of poor flesh.

What we consider imperfections to be remedied in the Bible were recognized by the Apostles, and by the chief of them, St. Peter, who writes, II. Pet. iii. 16: "Our dear brother Paul, according to the wisdom given him, has written to you; as also in all his Epistles; in which are certain things hard to be understood, which the unlearned and unstable wrest, as they do also the other Scriptures, to their own destruction." Here was room for depolarization, yet St. Peter did not take it in hand, neither should we desire scholars of perhaps greater knowledge but less wisdom to do so.

XX.

THE VULGATE AND THE REVISED PROTESTANT VERSION OF THE BIBLE.

In instituting here a comparison between the two approved and typical English Versions of the Bible as in use among Catholics and Protestants respectively, I have no intention to be aggressive or polemic. As from the first we have taken what may be called the common-sense point of view in judging the Bible as an historical work, which verifies its claims to be regarded as an organ communicating to us divine knowledge, so we proceed to make a brief suggestive examination of two English Bibles: one found in the homes of Catholics, the other in those of our Protestant friends and neighbors, many of whom believe with all sincerity that among the various doubts and difficulties of life they can consult no truer guide than that sacred volume.

Taking the two volumes as a whole, and considering only their general contents, there is but little difference between them. I compared them in a former chapter to the two American flags of North and South: viewed in themselves, these are both of the same origin, copied from the same pattern, and emblems, both, of American independence. Though they differ only in some detail that might escape the superficial observer, they nevertheless represent very widely different principles, for which the men of the South as of the North were willing to stake their lives. They might meet in friendly intercourse in all the walks of daily life, but if you ask a Union soldier to carry the Southern flag, he will say: No; for though it looks very much like my own, there is a difference, and that difference constitutes a vital principle with me.

Catholics have to make much the same answer when told that they might accept the Protestant Bible in their public relations with those who do not recognize the Catholic Church. The Catholic Church has the old Bible, as it came down the ages, complete and without changes. She has no reason to discard it, and she has good reason not to accept another Bible, though its English be sweeter and its periods fall upon the ear like the soft cadences of Southern army songs. We cannot sing from its tuneful pages, because it represents the principle of opposition to its original source and parent-stock, and no union can be effected except by the elimination of that principle.

Catholics claim that their Bible, in point of fidelity to the original—and this is the *essential* point when we speak of a translation of such a book—Catholics claim that their Bible, in point of fidelity to the original, is as superior to the Protestant English Bible of King James as it is, we admit, inferior in its English. "The translators of the Catholic Version considered it a lesser offence to violate some rules of grammar than to risk the sense of God's word for the sake of a fine period."[1]

What proof have we for such a claim? I answer that we have the strongest proof in the world which we could have on such a subject outside of a divine revelation, namely, the admission on the part of the guardians and translators themselves of the Protestant Bible. Now, when I say guardians and translators of the Protestant Bible, I do not mean merely the testimony of a few great authorities in the past or present who may have expressed their opinion as to the faults and defects of the latest English Protestant translation. That would not be fair. But I mean that the history itself of Protestant translations made since the days of King James, not to go back any farther, is a standing argument of the severest kind:

First, *against* the correctness of the *Protestant* English Versions; and,

Secondly, *for the* correctness of the *Catholic* English Version.

For if we compare the first Protestant English Version (which departed considerably from the received Catholic text of the Vulgate) with all the succeeding revisions made at various times by the English Protestants, we find that they have steadily returned towards the old Catholic Version. This is not only an improvement as

---

[1] Cf. a paper on the subject of the New Revision in the *Dublin Review*, 1881, vol. VI., ser. iii.

an approach to the Catholic teaching, but it is also a confession, however reluctantly made, of past errors on the part of former Protestant translators.

At the time of their separation from the Catholic Church the reformers, so-called, had to give reasons for their defection. They found fault with one doctrine or another in the old Catholic Church, such as the supremacy of the Roman Pontiff, the jurisdiction of bishops, the Holy Sacrifice, celibacy, confession, etc. To justify the rejection of these doctrines they must appeal to some authority: if not to the Pontiff, then to the king, or to the Bible, or to both simultaneously. But though the king might favor their novelties of doctrine inasmuch as they relieved his conscience of the reproach of disobedience to the Pontiff, who knew but one law of morals for the prince and the peasant, the Bible as hitherto read was against them. Now, Luther had given distracted Germany an example of what might be done in the way of whittling down the supernatural, and eliminating some of the irksome duties imposed by the old Church. He had made a new translation of the Bible, threw out passages, nay, whole books,[1] which did not meet his views, and added here and there a little word which did admirable service by setting him right with a world that for the most part could neither

---

[1] These books have been mostly retained in the Protestant Bible under the name of *Apocryphal*, *i. e.*, not inspired. The Church accepts and defines their inspiration, and in this is supported by the strong testimony of apostolic tradition.

read Hebrew nor Latin nor Greek, and trusted him for a learned translator.

In similar fashion an English translation had already been attempted by Wiclif about 1380, and almost simultaneously by Nicolas of Hereford. There existed in England at the time of Luther an edition of the Scriptures called the "great Bible." It was Catholic up to its fourth edition, that of 1541. Then, as is generally supposed, it was revised by the Elizabethan bishops in 1568, and in 1611, after a more lengthened revision, it appeared as a King James "Authorized Version." Since then various revisions and corrections of this Bible have been printed, each succeeding one eliminating some of the previous errors. Mr. Thomas Ward has made up an interesting book called "Errata—the truth of the English translations of the Bible examined," or "a treatise showing some of the errors that are found in the English translation of the Sacred Scriptures used by Protestants against such points of religious doctrine as are the subject of controversy between them and the members of the Catholic Church." Dr. Ward's book embraces a comparison between the Catholic English translation and the various Protestant versions up to the year 1683, for since then no changes were made in the English Protestant Bible called the authorized version until 1871, when the work of a new revision, published between 1881–85, was undertaken, which is not included in Dr. Ward's "Errata."

Why was this last revision made? Was not the King James version of 1611, for the most part, beautiful English? As to the rest, was it not for every Protestant an absolute, infallible rule of faith? The language was good, the truth still better; what need, then, was there to revise?

The revisers of 1881 tell us that the language of the old English version could be improved, and that they meant to improve it. The older translators, they say, "seem to have been guided by the feeling that their version would secure for the words they used a lasting place in the language; . . . but it cannot be doubted that the studied avoidance of uniformity in the rendering of the same words, even when occurring in the same context, is one of the blemishes in their work."

But are the changes of language or expression all that the reviewers of this infallible text-book aim at? No. Listen to what Dr. Ellicott in the Preface to the Pastoral Epistles says:

"It is vain to cheat our souls with the thought that these errors are either insignificant or imaginary. There *are* errors, there *are* inaccuracies, there *are* misconceptions, there *are* obscurities, not, indeed, so many in number or so grave in character as some of the forward spirits of our day would persuade us; but there *are* misrepresentations of the language of the Holy Ghost; and that man who, after being in any degree satisfied of this, permits himself to bow to the counsels of a timid or popular obstructiveness, or who, intellectually unable to test the truth of these allegations, nevertheless permits himself to denounce or deny them, will, if they be true, most surely at the dread day of final account have to sustain the tremendous charge of having dealt deceitfully with the inviolable Word of God."[1]

So this book, the infallible voice of God revealing His ways, this sole rule of faith for millions of Englishmen, and by which millions had lived and sworn and died during more than two centuries, had to be revised, not only as to the form, but in the matter also. Two committees were formed, about fifty of the members being from England, thirty from America—Presbyterians, Baptists, Methodists, etc. Cardinal Newman and Dr. Pusey were invited, but declined to attend. Mr. Vance Smith, a Unitarian, a distinguished scholar, but certainly no Christian, received a place in the New Testament committee. These gentlemen set to work in earnest to revise the Word of God and settle the Bible of the future. They had to consider the advance made in textual criticism represented by Lachmann, Scholz, Tregelles, Tischendorf, and Drs. Westcott and Hort.

They labored ten years and a half, as Dr. Ellicott assures us, " with thoroughness, loyalty to the authorized versions, and due recognition of the best judgment of antiquity. One of their rules, expressly laid down for their common guidance, was to introduce as few alter-

[1] "Pastoral Epistles," p. 13.

ations as possible into the text of the authorized version."

How many corrections, think you, were made in the New Testament alone? About 20,000, of which fifty per cent. are textual, that is "9 to every five verses of the Gospels, and 15 to every five in the Epistles." Besides these changes, which must be a shock to many an English Protestant who has accustomed himself by long reading of the Bible to believe in verbal inspiration, there are a number of omissions in the New Revised Text which in all amount to about 40 entire verses. It appears, then, that the King James Bible of some years ago has not been as most Protestants of necessity claimed for it—the pure, authentic, unadulterated Word of God. And if not, what guarantee have we that the promiscuous body of recent translators, however learned, withal not inspired, have given us that pure, authentic, unadulterated Word of God?

Let us glance over a few pages of the New Testament to see of what nature and of what importance, from a doctrinal point of view, are the changes made by the late revisers of the "Authorized (Protestant) Version."

In the first place, they have acknowledged the reading of I. Cor. xi. 27, regarding communion under one kind, by translating the Greek ἤ by *or*, and not by *and*, an error which had been repeated in all the Protestant translations since 1525, and which gave rise to endless abuse of the Catholic practice of giving the Blessed Sacrament to

The Vulgate and the Revised Protestant Version. 123

the laity under only one species. "Whosoever shall eat the bread *or* drink the cup" is the reading in the Greek as well as in the Latin Vulgate, and nothing but "theological fear or partiality," as Dean Stanley expressed it, could have warranted this mistranslation, which may be found in all the editions of 1526, 1538, 1562, 1568, 1577, 1579, 1611, etc.

But this is only one of many acts of justice which the learned revisers have done to Catholics by restoring the true reading; they have given us back the *altar* which, together with the Holy Sacrifice and confession and celibacy, had become obnoxious to the "reformers." We now read, I. Cor. x. 18, that "those that eat the hosts" are in "communion with the *altar*," where formerly they were only "partakers of the temple."

Having restored the Catholic practice of Holy Communion under one kind, and likewise the altar, we are not surprised that the "overseers" of the King James version should have become *bishops*, as in Acts xx. 28, although a good many of the *overseers* have been left in their places, possibly because the "elders" (Acts xv. 2; Tit. i. 5; I. Tim. v. 17 and 19, etc.) have not yet become *priests*, as they are in the Rhemish (Catholic) translation. However, the "elders" are likely to turn out priests at the next revision, because they are not only "ordained," but also "appointed," whereas in the old English revisions of 1562 and 1579 they were ordained elders "by election in every congregation," which is still done in

Protestant churches where there are no bishops, and even in some which have "overseers" with the honorary title of "bishop."

As to the celibacy question, the revisers have not thought fit to endorse it by translating ἀδελφὴν γυναῖκα a "woman," a sister; but they adhere to the old "wife," as Beza, in his translation, makes the Apostles go about with their "wives" (Acts i. 14).

In the matter of "confession" we have got a degree nearer to the old Catholic version and practice likewise. The Protestant reformers had no "sins" to confess; they had only "faults." Hence they translate St. James v. 16 by "confess your faults." But the revisers of 1881 found out that these "faults" were downright *sins*, and so they put it. Accordingly we find that the Apostles have power literally "to forgive" sins, whereas formerly, the sins being only faults, it was enough to have them "remitted," which means a sort of passive yielding or condoning on the part of the overseers in favor of repentant sinners, but did not convey the idea of a sacramental power "binding and loosening" in heaven as on earth.

Our dear Blessed Lady also receives some justice at the hands of the new translators. She is not simply "highly favored" as in the times of King James and ever since, but now is "endued with grace," though only in a footnote.

"It was expected," says an anonymous writer in the

The Vulgate and the Revised Protestant Version. 125

above cited article of the *Dublin Review*,[1] "that the revisers, in deference to modern refinement, would get rid of 'hell' and 'damnation,' like the judge who was said to have dismissed hell with costs. 'Damnation' and kindred words have gone. ... A new word, 'Hades,' Pluto's Greek name, has been brought into our language to save the old word 'hell' from overwork. The Rich Man is no longer in 'hell,' he is now '*in Hades;*' but he is still 'in torment.' So Hades must be Purgatory, and the revisers have thus moved Dives into Purgatory, and Purgatory into the Gospel. Dives will not object; but what will Protestants say?"

An important change has been introduced in their treatment of the Lord's Prayer. Protestants, for over three hundred years, have concluded that prayer with the words: "for Thine is the kingdom and the power and the glory forever." These words were to be found in St. Matt. vi. 13 according to the Protestant text. They were certainly wanting in St. Luke xi. 2, who also gives us the words of the "Our Father" with a very slight change of form. Catholics were reproached for not adding the 'doxology,' which proved to be a custom in the Greek Catholic Church, very much like our use of the "Glory be to the Father, and to the Son," etc., at the end of each psalm recited or sung at Vespers. Examination showed that the phrase "for Thine is the kingdom," etc., was to be found principally in versions

[1] Vol. VI., ser. III.

made by and for the Catholics of the Greek Church, and this explained how the same had crept into the copyists' Greek version. This fact is recognized at length in the late revision where the words are omitted from the text of St. Matthew, whilst a footnote states that "many authorities, some ancient, but with variations, add: 'for Thine is the kingdom and the glory forever.'"

The American revisers had made a number of very sensible suggestions, which would have brought the new Protestant version of the Bible still nearer to the old Catholic translation of Rheims and Douay; but their voice was not considered weighty enough, and Mr. Vance Smith openly blames the English committee on this score, saying that "they have not shown that judicial freedom from theological bias which was certainly expected from them." On the other hand, the American revisers showed their national spirit and liberality to a degree which must have horrified the orthodox members of the Anglican Community. The Americans "suggested the removal of all mention of the sin of heresy—heresies in their eyes being only 'factions.' They desired also that the Apostles and Evangelists should drop their title of Saint, and be content to be called plain John, and Paul, and Thomas. This resulted, no doubt, from their democratic taste for strict equality, and their hatred of titles even in the kingdom of heaven."[1]

[1] *Dublin Review, l. c.*

The Vulgate and the Revised Protestant Version. 127

After all this the principle of faith in the Bible alone became somewhat insecure, and we find the revisers making a silent concession on this point by allowing something to the Catholic principle of a living, perpetually transmitted *tradition*. St. Paul, who speaks of the *altar* and of *bishops*, and who allows *Communion under one kind*, and who had no wife, and wanted none (I. Cor. vii.), praises the Corinthians, not simply for keeping his "ordinances," as in the time of King James, but for keeping the *traditions* as he had delivered them to the Greek churches before he found opportunity to write to the Corinthians.

There is one other point of difference between the Catholic and Protestant Bibles to which it is instructive to call attention. It is in regard to the writing of proper names, especially in the Old Testament. Thus where we in the Catholic Bibles have *Nabuchodonosor* for the king of Babylon, son of Nabopollassar, the Protestant version has *Nebuchadnezzar;* where we have *Elias* and *Eliseus,* the Protestant version has *Elijah* and *Elisha,* and so forth regarding many Hebrew names of persons and places. You will ask whence the difference, and which is right?

The difference arises from the fact that the Protestant Version follows the present Hebrew text of the Bible, whilst the Catholic Version follows the Greek. Which is the safer to follow on such points as the pronunciation of proper names—the Hebrew or the Greek? You will say the Hebrew, but it is not so. The old Hebrew writing had, as I mentioned before, no vowels. Hence it could not be read by any one who had not heard it read in the schools of the rabbis. Some *six centuries after our Lord*, certain Jewish doctors who were called Masorets, anxious to preserve the traditional sounds of the Hebrew language, supplied vowels in the shape of points, which they placed under the square consonants, without disturbing the latter. Hence the present vowel system in Hebrew, or, in other words, the present pronunciation of Hebrew according to the reading of the Bible, is the work of men who relied for the pronunciation of words on a tradition which carried them back over many centuries, that is, from the time when Hebrew was a living language to about six hundred years after Christ. It is not difficult to imagine how in such a length of time the true pronunciation may have been lost or certainly modified in some cases; for though the Hebrew words were there on the paper, written in consonants of the old form, the pronunciation of the vowels must have been doubtful if resting on tradition alone, since the Hebrew had already ceased to be a living language for many centuries.

In the meantime, the true pronunciation of the Hebrew proper names could have been preserved in some of the translations made long before the Masoretic doctors supplied their vowel points. One of these translations from the Hebrew is the Greek Septuagint. It

The Vulgate and the Revised Protestant Version. 129

was made, as we have seen, in the time of Ptolemy, *i. e.*, some two and a half centuries before Christ. The learned Jews who made this translation knew perfectly well how the Hebrew of their day was pronounced, and we cannot suppose that they would mutilate the proper names of their mother tongue in the translation into Greek which, possessing written vowels, obliged them to express the full pronunciation of the persons and places which they transcribed.

Accordingly, we have two sources for our pronunciation of Hebrew proper names: one which dates from about the sixth or seventh century of the present era, when the Hebrew had become a dead language; and another, made about *nine hundred years earlier* by Jewish rabbis, who spoke the language perfectly well, and who could *express the pronunciation of proper names* accurately because they wrote in a language which had *written* vowels, and with which they were as conversant as with their own, the Hebrew.

Furthermore, we have other versions, made long before the Masoretic Doctors invented their vowel-points in order to fix the Hebrew pronunciation as they conceived it. Among these is the Latin Vulgate which, like the Greek of the Septuagint, should give us the correct pronunciation—because it was made by St. Jerome, who had studied the Hebrew and Chaldee in Palestine under a Jewish rabbi. He knew, therefore, the pronunciation of the Jews in his day (331–420), and there was no reason why he should not give it to us in his several different translations, whilst there might have been some cause why the Masoretic Jews who lived two or three centuries later should dislike to accept either the Greek or the Latin versions for an authority, because both versions were used and constantly cited by the Christians as proof that the Messiah had come.

Incidentally, the late archeological finds confirm this. Thus the name of Nabuchodonosor (IV. Kings xxiv. 1) (Protestant, Nebuchadnezzar), mentioned above as an example, reads in the cuneiform inscription of the Assyrian monument Nebukudursur, which is evidently the same form of vowel pronunciation as that employed in the Catholic version.

In comparing the two versions thus far little has been said as to the peculiar character or merits of the English Catholic version commonly called the Vulgate English or Douay Bible. But the main purpose of the present chapter has been attained by the necessary inference which the reader must have drawn, namely, that the old Catholic version is the more faithful, and that, after all, the Bible is not a safe guide without a Church to guard its integrity and to interpret its meaning.

But let me say just a word about the Vulgate. The Catholic Vulgate is practically the work of St. Jerome, and our English Catholic edition is made as literally as may be from this Latin Vulgate, "diligently compared with the Hebrew, Greek, and other editions in divers

The Vulgate and the Revised Protestant Version. 131

languages." The copies, most in use now, were made from an edition published by the English College at Rheims in 1582, and at Douay in 1609, revised by Dr. Challoner.

The need of a new revision has been recognized, and an effort to supply the want was made by the late Archbishop Kenrick, whose translation was recommended by the Council of Baltimore in 1858, although it has not been generally adopted. However, the changes to be made in the translation of the Catholic Bible in English cannot be very numerous nor affecting doctrines defined by the Church; nor is any accidental change of words or expressions so vital a matter to the Catholic mind as it must be with those who have but the Bible as their one primary rule of faith. So far Protestant revisions have done Catholics a service in removing by sucessive corrections one error after another from the "reformed" Bible, thus demonstrating the correctness of the old Vulgate; but they have also led Protestants to reflect seriously, and to realize that the "Bible only" principle is proved to be false and dangerous. They must see that the Scripture is powerless without the Church as the witness to its inspiration, the safeguard of its integrity, and the exponent of its meaning.

XXI.

THE POSITION OF THE CHURCH IN THE PRESENT STATE OF THE SCIENTIFIC CONTROVERSY REGARDING THE BIBLE.

In one of the old churches of Wales you may see the Ten Commandments written upon the wall, and beneath them the following inscription, the meaning of which, it is said, had for a long time remained a mystery to the people:

P R S V R Y P R F C T M N,
V R K P T H S P R C P T S T N.

Some one supplied the key to the interpretation by suggesting the letter E. Then everybody read the lines, and the old folks told their children, who inform the casual visitor that the strange letters plainly mean: *Persevere ye perfect men, ever keep these precepts ten.*

The inscription in the old Welsh church is a good illustration of the old text of the Bible, which had no vowels, no division of words and sentences. God gave the key to its meaning through an intelligent interpreter, and the men of learning supply the divisions—even in this sense that they sometimes dispute the place where to insert and where to omit the E.

The original obscurity has induced many to study the Bible, and the grand result of this study in our day has been to lead the great majority of scientific men, whether they are believers in the divine origin of the Book or not, to the conclusion that it is, to say the least, an historical monument of the highest antiquity, the contents of which have come down to us in that genuine and authentic form which is claimed for it; that is to say, that it has not been tampered with or falsified to such an extent as would render its statements materially other than they were from the beginning.

Tischendorf, one of the leading Biblical text critics in recent times, allows indeed some 30,000 variations for the New Testament alone in the different manuscripts of which we possess any trace. Although these variations are on the whole very slight, so as not to affect the genuineness of the Scripture documents, they establish the fact that we do not possess the text of the Bible in the *literal* form in which the inspired writers originally wrote it down.

Whatever changes have crept into the text of the Bible, through inadvertence of copyists or defective translations into other languages, it is a settled fact among Catholic divines that they do not affect the moral and dogmatic teaching of the Catholic Church. They regard either purely historical incidents or scientific facts, neither of which are the object of the doctrinal definitions or moral teachings of the Church. They are the proper subject for the study of human reason and investigation. Hence philological science may very becomingly occupy itself with the verbal criticism of the language and thought of the Bible. But the Catholic Church, as a teacher of religious truth, has an interest in these studies of verbal criticism in so far only as they may become a help or a hindrance to her legitimate activity of preaching and preserving the truth of Christianity. As a rule, the Church anticipates the dangerous issues arising from the misuse of such studies by deliberately defining not only the right use of the instruments employed for the purpose of criticism, but also what she herself deems the subject-matter lying outside of the domain of such criticism. Thus, in a negative way, she points out the field for the exercise of theories, or rather she defines the lines beyond which speculation may not safely go. The Church would have no end of tasks if she undertook to defend her position against the continuously proposed hypotheses by which any chance comer might venture to challenge her veracity or authority. Most theories are ephemeral; two, succeeding each other, are often mutually destructive. Prof. H. L. Hastings in his "Higher Criticism" tells us that since 1850 there have been published 747 theories, known to him, about the origin and authenticity of the Bible. Of these 747 theories he counts 608 as now defunct, and as the Professor wrote several years ago, we may assume that nearly all of the remaining 139 are dead by this time, although a few new ones have come in to take their place for a day.[1]

What, then, is the position of the Catholic Church, as limited by *positive definition*, with regard to the text of the Bible, by which she limits the aggressiveness of Biblical criticism?

The Catholic Church gives us a very ancient and well-attested text of the entire Bible in the Latin tongue, and in virtue of her commission to teach, which includes the right and duty to appoint the text-book for that teaching, she says: *The sacred Council of Trent, believing that it would be of great advantage to the Church of God to have it known which of the various Latin editions of the Bible is to be held authentic, hereby declares that the ancient edition commonly known as the Vulgate, which has been approved by the long-standing use of ages in the Church, is to be considered as the authentic Bible for official uses of teaching* (Trent, vi. 12).

You notice that the Council of Trent does not say that the Vulgate corresponds exactly to the literal original text, nor that it is the best of all known translations. The Council states only, but states explicitly, that the Vulgate edition of the Bible is a reliable source of the written revelation in matters of faith and morals. And the reason which the Council alleges for this preference of the Vulgate over other editions is its constant use for centuries in the Church; in other words, that it repre-

[1] See Hettinger's "Apologie," Preface xi.

sents the best tradition of the received text-form of the Sacred Scriptures. But the definition of the Council implies not only that the contents of the Vulgate in their entirety are reliable and authentic, but that each of its statements is authentic in its dogmatic contents, since the whole Vulgate, *i. e.*, in all its parts, is said to constitute a medium or instrument of official teaching in the Church. The declaration of the Council is regarding the *Latin* Vulgate; hence all translations must conform to *its* text, that is to say, the corrected text of 1592, called the Clementine recension.

It is noteworthy that, whilst the Church points out a text which is to be the official pattern in her liturgy and in the defence of Catholic teaching regarding faith and morals, she does not define anything regarding other texts or versions of the Bible. Neither the Hebrew nor the Greek texts are mentioned, although the Church gives to them, and the Coptic, Syrian, and Armenian versions, an implied approbation by tolerating their liturgical use in the Oriental churches.

What the Church has defined, therefore, regarding the Vulgate is this: It has declared its *dogmatic integrity*. This implies that the contents of the Vulgate give in their entirety and in their details a reliable version of the inspired text as an instrument of teaching Catholic truth and morals.

From a scientific point of view the Vulgate enjoys the advantage of being the oldest of all the Scriptural versions. In the Old Testament it represents a text more ancient than the Hebrew of the Masoretic doctors. The New Testament is likewise older than the oldest Greek text extant, as Lachmann in his critical edition has demonstrated. Moreover, its composition is the result of the best scientific apparatus of early Christian times, which St. Jerome possessed in a phenomenal degree, both as to his person and also as to the circumstances in which he was placed. Finally, it has an historical support of unequalled superiority, inasmuch as it has been from the beginning the means of Christianizing the nations of Europe.

All this is being verified, not only by textual critics, but by the more recent discoveries in the study of Christian paleography.

Such is the position in which scientific research finds the Church. The multiform theories about the Bible, and the various possible senses of its words and passages, only affect her in a limited degree. Catholic apologists are obliged to deal with these theories so far only as they affect the positive teaching of the Church in faith and morals, although the analogy of faith demands that the Catholic scientist test his opinions by weighty tradition and approved practice. Whilst the *dogmatic* integrity of the Sacred Scriptures is thus secured, the examination of the critical integrity of individual parts leaves a wide field open to Catholic Biblical students. The work done by non-Catholic scholars who have examined the Bible, either to bring out the verbal meaning of its text, or to verify some historical or philological hypothesis, is astounding. Catholic students owe a great debt to the first gleaners in this field; for though we have neither felt impelled to look for the rule of our faith in the Bible exclusively, nor always been inclined to accept the dicta regarding the literal sense of so sacred a document from the professors of philological discipline, we have incidentally profited by all these searchings. They have illustrated the excellence of our faith, both as a system and as a moral principle. They have thrown light upon problems of exegesis. All the doctrines and practices of the Catholic Church have found their confirmation in the analysis of Biblical terms as the result of textual criticism. The words of the Bible have been thrown into the crucible, and the gold of Catholic doctrine has been the outcome—purer, brighter, more refined, and still weighty. Each verified theory regarding the sense of old forgotten Hebrew terms has received the impress of Catholic approbation, and served to give the doctrine of the Church a more ready currency. Scientists, often reluctantly, are pointing out golden opportunities for Catholic students.

It does not come within our present scope to speak of the various methods employed by the science and art of Biblical criticism, nor to retail the separate results to which the inquiry into the authenticity (Higher Criticism) and the integrity and purity of the text

The Position of the Church. 139

(Lower Criticism) has led. The history of the New Testament, which is the best witness to the authenticity and integrity of the Old Testament books, provided we admit the divinity of Christ, which in its turn rests upon the strongest historic evidence, has received an immense amount of confirmatory argument in numerous discoveries of ancient documents. Within the last forty years have been found, among other valuable writings, the famous *Codex Sinaiticus* by Tischendorf (1859), one of the oldest Greek texts of the Bible. In 1875 Archbishop Briennios found in Constantinople the MS. Epistles of Clement of Rome, which not only confirm the apostolical writings and evangels as being received in the Church of his day, but furnish the oldest liturgical prayer and sermon of post-apostolic times. Another document of the same character, in Latin, was discovered by Morin in 1893. Next we have the celebrated *Diatessaron of Tatian,* the oldest gospel harmony in existence, which, known to Eusebius, but lost in the meantime, was recovered lately, with a parallel manuscript found in Egypt, and published last year in English. This takes us back to the time of St. Justin. Another most important find is the MS. of the so-called "Teaching of the Twelve Apostles." The document was discovered by Briennios, and published in 1883. It throws much light on the ecclesiastical discipline of the early Christian Church (about A. D. 120), speaks of the written Gospels, etc. Another valuable MS. (Syriac) was found in 1889 by Professor Harris. It is the "Apology of Aristides," brought from the convent of St. Catharine on Mt. Sinai, and dates about the year 140, as it is addressed to the Emperor Hadrian, and offers him the Christian Scriptures to read.

I pass over a host of other important finds of the same nature, of unquestioned authenticity, which carry us back to the apostolic age.

XXII.

MYSTERIOUS CHARACTERS.

Whilst Biblical criticism and constantly increasing discoveries of new treasures, such as we mentioned in the last chapter, are adding their approving light to the ancient and unchanged traditions of the Catholic Church regarding the Bible and its exegesis, the finds of archeology are confirming the statements of the Bible, especially the Old Testament history, with an accuracy which forces even the infidel scientist to bear witness to the historical truth of the inspired records.

A century ago Biblical antiquity received its side-lights, for the most part, from rabbinical literature, and from newly-discovered methods of interpreting those classics which dealt with the Oriental world incidentally. But in modern times an immense literary field has been opened by the discovery of ancient monuments in Egypt, Assyria, Babylonia, Syria, Asia Minor, Palestine, and the surrounding countries. These monuments place us in position to trace the condition of these nations to very remote periods, and give us a key to the explanation of the Biblical documents. Extraordinary labor, coupled with all-sided knowledge, a refined method of observation, and untiring patience, have made it possible to read the hieroglyphics and the so-called cuneiform inscriptions. It is interesting to trace the gradual progress by which definite results were attained in deciphering certain inscriptions whose language was entirely unknown to any living man. I may be allowed to give here an illustration, taken from Mr. Sayce's excellent little work, "Fresh Lights on Ancient Monuments," in which he describes the manner of unravelling the mysterious threads of the old Persian script:

"Travellers had discovered inscriptions engraved in cuneiform, or, as they were also termed, arrow-headed, characters on the ruined monuments of Persepolis and other ancient sites in Persia. Some of these monuments were known to have been erected by the Achæmenian princes—Darius, the son of Hystaspes, and his successors—and it was therefore inferred that the inscriptions also had been carved by order of the same kings. The inscriptions were in three different systems of cuneiform writing; and, since the three kinds of inscription were always placed side by side, it was evident that they represented different versions of the same text. The subjects of the Persian kings belonged to more than one race, and, just as in the present day a Turkish pasha in the East has to publish an edict in Turkish, Arabic, and Persian, if it is to be understood by all the populations under his charge, so the Persian kings were obliged to use the language and system of writing peculiar to each of the nations they governed whenever they wished their proclamations to be read and understood by them.

"It was clear that the three versions of the Achæmenian inscriptions were addressed to the three chief populations of the Persian empire, and that the one that invariably came first was composed in ancient Persian, the language of the sovereign himself. Now this Persian version happened to offer the decipherer less difficulties than the two others which accompanied it. The number of distinct characters employed in writing it did not exceed forty, while the words were divided from one another by a slanting wedge. Some of the words contained so many characters that it was plain that these latter must denote letters, and not syllables, and that consequently the Persian cuneiform system must have consisted of an alphabet, and not of a syllabary. It was further plain that the inscriptions had to be read from left to right, since the ends of all the lines were exactly underneath one another on the left side, whereas they terminated irregularly on the right; indeed, the last line sometimes ended at a considerable distance from the right-hand extremity of the inscription.

"The clue to the decipherment of the inscriptions was first discovered by the successful guess of a German scholar, Grotefend. Grotefend noticed that the inscriptions generally began with three or four words, one of which varied, while the others remained unchanged. The variable word had three forms, though the same form always appeared on the same monument. Grotefend, therefore, conjectured that this word represented the name of a king, the words which followed it being the royal titles. One of the supposed names appeared much oftener than the others, and, as it was too short for Artaxerxes and too long for Cyrus, it was evident that it must stand either for Darius or for Xerxes. A study of the classical authors showed Grotefend that certain of the monuments on which it was found had been constructed by Darius, and he accordingly gave to the characters composing it the values required for spelling 'Darius' in its old Persian form. In this way he succeeded in obtaining conjectural values for six cuneiform letters. He now turned to the second royal name, which also appeared on several monuments, and was of much the same length as that of Darius. This could only be Xerxes; but if so, the fifth letter composing it (r) would necessarily be the same as the third letter in the name of Darius. This proved to be the case, and thus afforded the best possible evidence that the German scholar was on the right track.

"The third name, which was much longer than the other two, differed from the second chiefly at the beginning, the latter part of it resembling the name of Xerxes. Clearly, therefore, it could be nothing else than Artaxerxes, and that it actually was so was rendered certain by the fact that the second character composing it was that which had the value of *r*.

"Grotefend now possessed a small alphabet, and with this he proceeded to read the word which always followed the royal name, and therefore probably meant 'king.' He found that it closely resembled the word which signified 'king' in Zend, the old language of the Eastern Persians, which was spoken in one part of Persia at the same time that Old Persian, the language of the Achæmenian princes, was spoken in another. There could, consequently, be no further room for doubt that he had really solved the great problem, and discovered the key to the decipherment of the cuneiform texts.

"But he did little further himself towards the completion of the work, and it was many years before any real progress was made with it. Meanwhile, the study of Zend had made great advances, more especially in the hands of Burnouf, who eventually turned his attention to the cuneiform inscriptions. But it is to Burnouf's pupil, Lassen, as well as to Sir Henry Rawlinson, that the decipherment of these inscriptions owes its final completion. The discovery of the list of Persian satrapies in the inscription of Darius at Naksh-i-Rustem, and above all the copy of the long inscription of Darius on the rock of Behistum, made by Sir H. Rawlinson, enabled these scholars independently of one another to construct an alphabet which differed only in the value assigned to a single character, and, with the help of the cognate Zend and Sanskrit, to translate the language so curiously brought to light. The decipherment of the Persian cuneiform texts thus became an accomplished fact ; what was next needed was to decipher the two versions which were inscribed at their side.

"But this was no easy task. The words in them were not divided from one another, and the characters of which they were composed were exceedingly numerous. With the assistance, however, of frequently recurring proper names, even these two versions gradually yielded to the patient skill of the decipherer; and it was then discovered that while one of them represented an agglutinative language, such as that of the Turks or Fins, the other was in a dialect which closely resembled the Hebrew of the Old Testament. The monuments found almost immediately afterwards in Assyria and Babylonia by Botta and Layard soon made it clear to what people this dialect must have belonged. The inscriptions of Nineveh turned out to be written in the same language and form of cuneiform script; and it must therefore have been for the Semitic population of Assyria and Babylonia that the kings of Persia had caused one of the versions of their inscriptions to be drawn up. This version served as a starting-point for the decipherment of the texts which the excavations in Assyria had brought to light."

In this way results which stood the test of severe criticism were obtained until the most difficult inscriptions have become a comparatively open book to the historian of to-day. Thus it has come about that, as Prof. Ira Price says: "Since 1850 the Old Testament has been gradually appearing in the ever-brightening and brighter light of contemporaneous history. The new light now pours in upon it from all sides. It is the one history made rich by that of all its neighbors. Israel is the one people whose part in the drama of ancient nations is just beginning to be understood. . . . The cuneiform letters discovered at Tel el-Amarna in Egypt, in 1887, have opened up new territory in the fifteenth century, B. C. They are despatches and official communications sent by a large number of rulers, kings, and governors, mainly of countries and provinces and cities of Southwestern Asia, to the king of Egypt. These documents disclose a marvellously advanced stage of development, intellectually, politically, and socially, among the people who were soon to be Israel's nearest neighbors. They formed the early background of Israel's settlement in Canaan, and prepare us for no surprises in Israel's growth. In fact, we see that Joshua and his army actually settled in a land of cities and fortresses, already containing many of the elements of civilization, but sadly reduced by internal and external warfare."

The labor of the excavator in the Biblical countries, such as the unearthing of the immense library of brick tablets in the neighborhood of Nineveh, and the result of new discoveries which the ground of Palestine, so long and strangely neglected, promises to yield, widen the field of Biblical research immensely, and from it all we may with perfect assurance look for fresh arguments in behalf of the authenticity and substantial integrity of the Sacred Scriptures. At the same time the interpretation of many of its passages, now obscure, will become clearer in the light of contemporary history.

Surely this is a hopeful sign, and should encourage us in the study of the Bible, which is on so many accounts a source of intellectual pleasure, of abiding peace of heart, and of that high moral refinement which comes from contact with noble minds. There are none better on earth than the sacred writers—men who walked and spoke with God, and whose living contact we may enjoy in the participation of that celestial inspiration which breathes through their writings.

CONCLUSION.

The foregoing chapters are nothing more than a brief illustration of the principles laid down by the Sovereign Pontiff, Leo XIII., in his Encyclical Letter "On the Study of the Sacred Scriptures."[1] The careful reading of this Letter must convince us how important a part the study of the Bible has always played in the Church. The conclusions of Leo XIII. are not of yesterday, nor does he claim them as of his own invention. He cites the Fathers and Doctors of the Church, and the Decrees of Councils, from Antioch to Trent and the Vatican, as witnesses to the fact that all Catholic teaching rests upon the Sacred Scriptures as one of the two great foundation stones which support the grand archway leading into the domain of divine truth. God, in order that He may reveal Himself to man, sends His messengers, the Prophets and the Apostles, to announce with living voice His promises and His judgments; then, as if to confirm their mission for all time to come, He bids them take a letter, written by Himself, and addressed "to the human race on its pilgrimage afar from its fatherland" (Encycl.). That letter is the Holy Scripture. "To understand and to explain it there is always required the 'coming' of the same Holy Spirit" who was to abide with the Church. And she, "by her admirable

[1] Litteræ Encyclicæ, "Providentissimus Deus," Nov. 17, A. D.1893.

laws and regulations, has always shown herself solicitous that the celestial treasure of the Sacred Book . . . should not be neglected" (Ibid.). If men have grown remiss at any time in the use of that heavenly gift, it cannot be said that the Church failed to keep before them its admirable utility. "She has arranged that a considerable portion of it should be read, and with pious mind considered by all her ministers in the daily office of the sacred psalmody." For centuries past the solemn promise of every ordained priest throughout the Catholic world to recite each day the Hours of the Breviary testifies to the constant practice of not only reading, but meditating a fixed portion of the Scriptures, so that under this strictest of his priestly obligations he has practically completed the entire sacred volume within the limit of each ecclesiastical year. "She has strictly commanded that her children shall be fed with the saving word of the Gospel, at least on Sundays and on solemn feasts." If these laws and this practice receive a fresh impulse from the Sovereign Pontiff in our day, it is because there have arisen men who teach that the Sacred Scriptures are the work of mere human industry, that they contain only fables, which have no claim to be respected as coming from God. "They deny that there is any such thing as divine revelation, or inspiration, or Holy Scripture at all: They see in these histories only forgeries and falsehoods of men. . . . The prophecies and the oracles of God are to them either predictions made up after the event, or forecasts formed by the light of nature. The miracles and manifestations of God's power are not what they profess to be, but are either startling effects which are not beyond the force of nature, or else mere tricks and myths. The Gospels and apostolic writings are not, they say, the work of the authors to whom they are assigned " (Ibid.). To confute these errors Leo bids us engage voice and pen. In the limited space allowed us we have only been able to indicate the arguments which prove the historical authenticity and the essentially divine character which points to the true origin of the Sacred Text, and at the same time to lead the earnest student into the way of reading with pleasure and profit the grandest of all written works.

THE END.

APPENDIX.

Encyclical Letter of Leo XIII.
ON
THE STUDY OF THE SACRED SCRIPTURES.

To Our Venerable Brethren, all Patriarchs, Primates, Archbishops, and Bishops of the Catholic World, in grace and communion with the Apostolic See.

LEO P. P. XIII.

VENERABLE BRETHREN,
Health and Apostolic Benediction.

The God of all Providence, who in the wondrous counsel of His love raised the human race in its beginning to participation of the divine nature, and afterwards delivered it from universal guilt and ruin, restoring it to its primitive dignity, has, in consequence, bestowed upon man a singular safeguard—making known to him, by supernatural means, the hidden mysteries of His divinity, His wisdom, and His mercy. Although in divine revelation some things are comprehended which are not beyond the reach of human reason, they are made the objects of revelation in order that all may come to know them with facility, certainty, and freedom from all error. It is not, however, on this account that revelation can be said to be absolutely necessary; but because God of His infinite goodness has ordained man to a supernatural end. This supernatural revelation, according to the belief of the universal Church, is contained both in unwritten Tradition and in written Books. These are called sacred and canonical because, being written under the inspiration of the Holy Ghost, they have God for their author, and as such have been delivered to the Church. This belief has been perpetually held and professed by the Church with regard to the Books of both Testaments. There are well-known documents of the gravest character, coming down to us from the earliest times, which proclaim that God, who spoke first by the Prophets, then by Himself, and thereafter by the Apostles, composed the Canonical Scriptures. These are divine oracles and utterances—a Letter, written by our heavenly Father, and transmitted by the sacred writers to the human race on its pilgrimage afar from its fatherland. If, then, such and so great is the excellence and the dignity of the Scriptures that God Himself has, as the author of them, composed them, and that they treat of God's deepest mysteries, counsels, and works, it follows that the branch of sacred theology which is concerned with the defence and interpretation of these divine books must be most excellent and in the highest degree profitable.

Now We, who by the help of God, and not without fruit, have by frequent letters and exhortation endeavored to promote other branches of study, which seemed well fitted for advancing the glory of God and contributing to the salvation of souls, have for a long time cherished the desire to give an impulse to the most noble study of the Sacred Scriptures, and to impart to it a direction which is suitable to the needs of the present day. The solicitude of the Apostolic office naturally urges, and even compels Us, not only to desire that this grand source of Catholic revelation should be made more safely and abundantly accessible to the flock of Jesus Christ, but also to prevent it from being in any way violated, on the part either of those who impiously and openly assail the Scriptures, or of those who are led astray into fallacious and imprudent novelties.

Appendix.

We are not ignorant, indeed, Venerable Brethren, that there are Catholics not a few, men abounding in talent and learning, who do devote themselves with alacrity to the defence of the Divine Books, and to making them better known and understood. But while giving to these men the commendation which they deserve for their labor and the fruits of it, We cannot but earnestly exhort others also, from whose skill and piety and learning we have a right to expect the very best results, to give themselves to the same most praiseworthy work. It is Our wish and fervent desire to see an increase in the number of approved and unwearying laborers in the cause of Holy Scripture; and more especially that those whom Divine Grace has called to Holy Orders should, day by day, as is most meet, display greater diligence and industry in reading, meditating, and explaining it.

Among the reasons for which this study is so worthy of commendation—in addition to its own excellence and to the homage which we owe to God's word—the chief reason of all is the manifold benefit of which it is the source. This we know will flow therefrom on the most certain testimony of the Holy Ghost Himself, who says: "All Scripture, inspired of God, is profitable to teach, to reprove, to correct, to instruct in justice, that the man of God may be perfect, furnished to every good work." That such was the purpose of God in giving the Scriptures to men is shown by the example of Christ our Lord and of His Apostles. He who obtained authority by miracles, merited belief by authority, and by belief drew to Himself the multitude, was accustomed in the exercise of His Divine Mission to appeal to the Scriptures. He uses them at times to prove that He was sent by God, and that He is God. From them He draws arguments for the instruction of His disciples and the confirmation of His doctrine. He vindicates them from the calumnies of objectors. He quotes them against Sadducees and Pharisees. He retorts from them upon

Satan himself, when he impudently dares to tempt Him. At the close of His life His utterances are from Holy Scripture. It is the Scripture which He expounds to His disciples after His resurrection, and during all the time till He ascends to the glory of His Father. Faithful to His precepts, the Apostles, although He Himself granted "signs and wonders to be done by their hands," nevertheless used with the greatest efficacy the sacred writings, in order to persuade the nations everywhere of the wisdom of Christianity, to break down the obstinacy of the Jews, and to suppress the outbursts of heresy. This is manifest in their discourses, especially in those of St. Peter. These were almost woven from sayings of the Old Testament, which made in the strongest manner for the new dispensation. We find the same thing in the Gospels of St. Matthew and St. John, and in the Catholic Epistles. Most remarkably of all is it to be found in the words of him who boasts that he learned the law at the feet of Gamaliel, in order that, being armed with spiritual weapons, he might afterwards say with confidence: "The weapons of our warfare are not carnal, but mighty unto God."

Let all, therefore, especially the novices of the ecclesiastical army, understand how much the divine Books should be esteemed, and with what determination and reverence they should approach this great arsenal of heavenly arms. Those whose duty it is to handle Catholic doctrine before either the learned or the unlearned will nowhere find more ample matter or more abundant exhortation, whether on the subject of God, the supreme and all perfect Good, or of the works which display His glory and His love. Nowhere is there anything more full or more express on the subject of the Saviour of the human race than that which is to be found throughout the Bible. St. Jerome has rightly said "ignorance of the Scripture is ignorance of Christ." In its pages His Image stands out as it were alive and breathing; diffusing everywhere consolation in trouble, encouragement to virtue, and attraction to the love of God. As regards the Church, her institutions, her nature, her functions, and her gifts, we find in Holy Scripture so many references, and so many ready and convincing arguments, that, as St. Jerome again most truly says: "A man who is thoroughly grounded in the testimonies of the Scriptures is a bulwark of the Church." If we come to moral formation and to discipline, an apostolic man finds in the sacred writings abundant and most excellent aid, precepts full of holiness, exhortations framed with sweetness and force, shining examples of every kind of virtue, and, finally, the promise of eternal reward, and the threat of eternal punishment, uttered in weightiest terms, in God's name and in God's own words.

This peculiar and singular power of the Scriptures, springing from the inspiration of the Holy Ghost, adds to the authority of the sacred orator, fills him with apostolic liberty of speech, and communicates to him a forcible and convincing eloquence. Those who infuse into their speech the spirit and strength of the Word of God speak, "not in words only, but in power also, and in the Holy Ghost, and in much fulness." Hence those preachers are foolish and improvident who, in preaching religion and proclaiming the precepts of God, use no words but those of human science and human prudence, trusting to their own reasonings rather than to those that are divine. Their discourses may be glittering with lights, but they must be cold and feeble, for they are without the fire of the utterance of God. They must fall far short of that power which the speech of God possesses. "The Word of God is living and effectual, and more piercing than any two-edged sword; and reaching unto the division of the soul and the spirit." All the more far-seeing are agreed that there is in the Holy Scriptures an eloquence that is marvellous in its variety and richness, and that is worthy of the loftiest themes. This St. Augustine thoroughly comprehended, and this he has abundantly set forth. It is confirmed also by the best of the preachers of all ages. They have gratefully acknowledged that they owed their repute chiefly to assiduous familiarity with the Bible, and to devout meditation on the truths which it contains.

The Holy Fathers well knew all this by practical experience. They never cease to extol the Sacred Scripture and its fruits. In innumerable passages of their writings we find them applying to it such phrases as—"an inexhaustible treasury of heavenly doctrine," or "an everflowing fountain of salvation," or as "fertile pastures and most lovely gardens, in which the flock of the Lord is marvellously refreshed and delighted." Let us listen to the words of St. Jerome, in his Epistle to the cleric Nepotian: "Often read the divine Scriptures; yea, let holy reading be always in thy hand; study that which thou thyself must preach. . . . Let the speech of the priest be ever seasoned with Scriptural reading." St. Gregory the Great, than whom no man has more admirably described the functions of the pastors of the Church, writes in the same sense: "Those," he says, "who are zealous in the work of preaching, must never cease from study of the written word of God." St. Augustine, however, warns us that " vainly does the preacher utter the word of God exteriorly unless he listens to it interiorly." St. Gregory instructs sacred orators "first, to find in Holy Scripture the knowledge of themselves, and then to carry it to others, lest in reproving others they forget themselves." This had already, after the example and teaching of Christ Himself, who "began to do and to teach," been uttered far and wide by an apostolic voice. It was not to Timothy alone, but to the whole order of the clergy, that the command was addressed: "Take heed to thyself and to doctrine; be earnest in them. In doing this thou shalt save both thyself and them that hear thee." For the saving and for the perfection, both of ourselves and of others, we have at hand the very best of aids in the Sacred Scriptures, and most abundantly in the Book of Psalms. Those alone will, however, find it who bring to the divine oracles not only a docile and attentive mind, but a habit also of will which is both pious and without reserve. The Sacred Scripture is not to be regarded like an ordinary book. Dictated by the Holy Ghost, it contains matters of the most grave importance, which in many instances are difficult and obscure. To understand and to explain them there is always required the "coming" of the same Holy Spirit; that is to say, His light and His grace. These, as the Royal Psalmist so frequently insists, are to be sought by humble prayer, and to be preserved by holiness of life.

It is in this that the watchful care of the Church shines forth conspicuously. By her admirable laws and regulations she has always shown herself solicitous that the celestial treasure of the Sacred Books, so bountifully bestowed upon man by the Holy Spirit, should not lie neglected. She has arranged that a considerable portion of them should be read, and with pious mind considered by all her ministers in the daily office of the sacred psalmody. She has ordered that in cathedral churches, in monasteries, and in convents of other regulars, which are places most fit for study, they shall be expounded and interpreted by capable men. She has strictly commanded that her children shall be fed with the saving word of the Gospel at least on Sundays and on solemn feasts. Moreover, it is owing to the wisdom and the diligence of the Church that there has always been, continued from century to century, that cultivation of Sacred Scripture which has been so remarkable and which has borne such ample fruit.

And here, in order to strengthen Our teaching and

Our exhortations, it is well to recall how, from the first beginnings of the Christian religion, so many who have been renowned for holiness of life and for sacred learning have given their deep and most constant attention to Holy Scripture. If we consider the immediate disciples of the Apostles, St. Clement of Rome, St. Ignatius of Antioch, and St. Polycarp—or the Apologists, such as St. Justin and St. Irenæus, we find that in their letters and in their books, whether in defence of the Catholic faith or in commendation of it, they draw faith and strength and unction mainly from the word of God. When there arose, in various Episcopal Sees, catechetical and theological schools, of which the most celebrated were those of Alexandria and of Antioch, there was little taught in those schools but what consisted in the reading, the unfolding, and the defence of the divine written word. From these schools came forth numbers of Fathers and of writers whose laborious studies and admirable writings have justly merited for the three following centuries the appellation of the golden age of biblical exegesis.

In the Eastern Church, the greatest name of all is Origen. He was a man remarkable alike for quickness of genius and for persevering labor. From his numerous writings and his immense work of the *Hexapla* almost all who came after him have drawn. Others who have widened the field of this science may also be named. Among the more excellent, Alexandria could boast of Clement and Cyril; Palestine, of Eusebius and the other Cyril; Cappadocia, of Basil the Great and the two Gregories, Nazianzen and Nyssene; and Antioch, of St. John Chrysostom, in whom skill in this learning was rivalled by the splendor of his eloquence.

In the Western Church there were many names as great: Tertullian, Cyprian, Hilary, Ambrose, Leo the Great, Gregory the Great; most famous of all, Augustine and Jerome. Of these two the former was marvellously acute in penetrating the sense of God's word, and most fertile in the use that he made of it for the promotion of Catholic truth. The latter has received from the Church, by reason of his pre-eminent knowledge of Scripture and the greatness of his labors in promoting its use, the name of the "Great Doctor."

From this period, down to the eleventh century, although biblical studies did not flourish with the same vigor and with the same fruitfulness as before, they nevertheless did flourish, and that principally through the instrumentality of the clergy. It was their care and solicitude that selected the most fruitful of the things which the ancients had left behind them, placed these in digested order, and published them with additions of their own—as did Isidore of Seville, Venerable Bede, and Alcuin, among the most prominent. It was they who illustrated the sacred pages with "glosses," or short commentaries, as we see in Walafrid Strabo and Anselm of Laon, or who expended fresh labor in securing their integrity, as did Peter Damian and Lanfranc.

In the twelfth century many took up with great success the allegorical exposition of Scripture. In this Bernard is easily pre-eminent. His writings, it may be said, are Scripture all through. With the age of the scholastics there came fresh and fruitful progress in the study of the Bible. That the scholastics were solicitous about the genuineness of the Latin version is evident from the *Correctoria Biblica*, or list of emendations, which they have left behind them. They expended, however, more of their study and of their industry on interpretation and on explanation. To them we owe the accurate and clear distinction, such as had not been given before, of the various senses of the sacred words; the weight of each word in the balance of theology; the division of books into parts, and the summaries of the various parts; the investigation of the purpose of the writers, and the unfolding of the necessary connection of one sentence with another. No man can fail to see the amount of light which was thus shed on the more obscure passages. The abundance of their Scriptural learning is to be seen both in their theological treatises and in their commentaries. In this Thomas of Aquin bears the palm.

When Our predecessor, Clement V., established chairs of Oriental literature in the Athenæum at Rome, and in the principal Universities of Europe, our students began to labor more minutely on the original text of the Bible, as well as on the Latin version. The revival amongst us of Greek learning, and, much more, the happy invention of the art of printing, gave the strongest impetus to the study of Holy Scripture. In a brief space of time innumerable editions, especially of the Vulgate, poured from the press, and were spread throughout the Catholic world; so honored and loved were the divine volumes during that very period against which the enemies of the Church direct their calumnies.

Nor must we forget how many learned men there were, chiefly among the religious orders, who did excellent work for the Bible between the dates of the Councils of Vienne and Trent. These men, by employment of modern means and appliances, and by contribution of their own genius and learning, not only added to the rich stores of ancient times, but prepared the way for the pre-eminence of the succeeding century—the century which followed the Council of Trent. It then seemed almost as if the great age of the Fathers had returned. It is well known, and We recall it with pleasure, that Our predecessors from Pius IV. to Clement VIII. caused to be prepared the celebrated editions of the Vulgate and the Septuagint, which, having been published by the command and authority of Sixtus V. and of the same Clement, are now in common use. At this time, moreover, were carefully brought out various other ancient versions of the Bible, and the Polyglots of Antwerp and of

Paris, most important for the investigation of the true meaning of the text. There is not any one Book of either Testament which did not find more than one expositor, nor is there any grave question which did not profitably exercise the ability of many inquirers. Among these there are not a few—more especially of those who made most study of the Fathers—who have made for themselves names of renown. From that time forward the labor and solicitude of our students have never been wanting. As time has gone on, eminent scholars have carried on biblical study with success. They have defended Holy Scripture against the cavils of *rationalism* with the same weapons of philology and kindred sciences with which it had been attacked. The calm and fair consideration of what has been said will clearly show that the Church has never failed in any manner of provision for bringing the fountains of the Divine Scripture in a wholesome way within reach of her children, and that she has ever held fast and exercised the guardianship divinely bestowed upon her for its protection and glory. She has never, therefore, required, nor does she now require, any stimulation from without.

We must now, Venerable Brethren, as Our purpose demands, impart to you such counsels as seem best suited for carrying on successfully the study of biblical science. We must, in the first place, have a clear idea of the kind of men whom we have to oppose, their tactics and their weapons.

In earlier times the contest was chiefly with those who, relying on private judgment and repudiating the divine tradition and the teaching authority of the Church, held the Scriptures to be the one and only source of revelation and the final appeal in matters of Faith. Now, we have to meet the Rationalists, the true children and heirs of the older heretics. Trusting in their turn to their own judgment, they have rejected even the scraps and remnants of Christian belief handed down to them from their fathers. They deny that there is any such thing as divine revelation, or inspiration, or Holy Scripture at all. They see in these histories only forgeries and falsehoods of men. They set down the Scripture narratives as stupid fables or lying tales. The prophecies and the oracles of God are to them either predictions made up after the event, or forecasts formed by the light of nature. The miracles and manifestations of God's power are not what they profess to be, but are either startling effects which are not beyond the forces of nature, or else mere tricks and myths. The Gospels and apostolic writings are not, they say, the work of the authors to whom they are assigned. These detestable errors, whereby they think to destroy the truth of the divine Books, are obtruded on the world as the peremptory pronouncements of a newly-invented " free science." This science, however, is so far from final that they are perpetually modifying and supplementing it. There are some of them who, notwithstanding their impious opinions and utterances about God and His Christ, the Gospels, and the rest of Holy Scripture, would fain be regarded as being theologians and Christians and men of the Gospel. They attempt to disguise under such names of honor their rashness and their insolence. To them we must add not a few professors of other sciences who approve and sustain their views, and are egged on to attack the Bible by intolerance of revelation. It is deplorable to see this warfare becoming from day to day more widespread and more ruthless. It is sometimes men of learning and judgment who are assailed; but these have little difficulty in standing on their guard. The efforts and the arts of the enemy are chiefly directed against the more ignorant masses of the people. These men diffuse their deadly poison by means of books and pamphlets and newspapers. They spread it by means of addresses and of conversations. They are found everywhere. They are in possession of numerous schools for the young, wrested from the guardianship of the Church. In these schools, by means of ridicule and scurrilous jesting, they pervert the credulous and unformed minds of the young to contempt of Scripture. Should not these things, Venerable Brethren, stir up and set on fire the heart of every Pastor, so that to this " knowledge, falsely so called," may be opposed the ancient and true science which the Church, through the Apostles, has received from Christ, and that the Sacred Scriptures may find champions that are strong for so great a struggle?

Let our first care, then, be to see that in Seminaries and Academical foundations the study of Holy Scripture is placed on such a footing as both the importance of it and the circumstances of the time demand. With this view, that which is of first importance is a wise selection of professors. Teachers of Sacred Scripture are not to be appointed at hap-hazard out of the crowd. They must be men whose character and fitness have been proved by great love of, and long familiarity with, the Bible, and by the learning and study which befits their office.

It is of equal importance to provide in due time for a continuous succession of such teachers. It will be well, wherever this can be done, to select young men of promise, who have studied their theology with distinction, and to set them apart exclusively for Holy Scripture, affording them time and facilities for still fuller study. Professors thus chosen and appointed may enter with confidence on the task that is set before them. That they may be at their best, and bear all the fruit that is possible, there are some other hints which We may somewhat more fully set before them.

At the commencement of a course of Holy Scripture, let the professor strive earnestly to form the judgment of the young beginners, so as to train them equally to defend the sacred writings and to penetrate their meaning. This is the object of the treatise which is called

"Introduction to the Bible." Here the student is taught how to prove its integrity and authority, how to investigate and ascertain its true sense, and how to meet and refute all captious objections. It is needless to insist on the importance of making these preliminary studies in an orderly and thorough way, in the company and with the aid of Theology. The whole of the subsequent course will rest on the foundation thus laid, and will be luminous with the light which has been thus acquired.

Next, the teacher will turn his earnest attention to that most fruitful branch of Scripture science which has to do with interpretation. Therein is imparted the method of using the word of God for the promotion of religion and of piety. We are well aware that neither the extent of the matter nor the time at disposal allows every single Book of the Bible to be separately studied in the schools. The teaching, however, should result in a definite and ascertained method of interpretation. Hence the professor should at once avoid giving a mere taste of every Book, and the equal mistake of dwelling at too great length on merely a part of some one Book. If most schools cannot do what is done in the larger institutions,—that is, take the students through the whole of one or two Books continuously, and with some considerable development—yet at least those parts which are selected for interpretation should be treated with some fulness. In this way the students may be attracted, and learn from the sample that is set before them to love and read the rest in the course of their after lives. The professor, following the tradition of antiquity, will use the Vulgate as his text. The Council of Trent has decreed that "in public lectures, disputations, preaching, and exposition," the Vulgate is the "authentic" version; and this is the existing custom of the Church. At the same time, the other versions which Christian antiquity has approved and used should not be neglected, more especially the more ancient MSS. Although the meaning of the Hebrew and the Greek is substantially rendered by the Vulgate, nevertheless, wherever there may be ambiguity or want of clearness, the "examination of older tongues," to quote St. Augustine, will be of service. In this matter we need hardly say that the greatest prudence is required, for the "office of a commentator," as St. Jerome says, " is to set forth not that which he himself would prefer, but that which his author says." The question of "readings" having been, when necessary, carefully discussed, the next thing is to investigate and expound the meaning. The first counsel to be here given is this: that the more our adversaries strive in the contrary direction, so much the more solicitously should we adhere to the received and approved canons of interpretation. Hence, while weighing the meanings of words, the connection of ideas, the parallelism of passages, and the like, we should by all means make use of external illustrations drawn from other cognate learning. This should, however, be done with caution, so as not to bestow on such questions more labor and time than that which is spent on the Sacred Books themselves, and not to overload the minds of the students with a mass of information which will be rather a hindrance than a help.

The professor may now safely pass on to the use of Scripture in matters of Theology. Here it must be observed that, in addition to the usual reasons which make ancient writings more or less difficult to understand, there are some which are peculiar to the Sacred Books. The language of the Bible is employed to express, under the inspiration of the Holy Ghost, many things which are beyond the powers and scope of human reason—that is to say, divine mysteries and many matters which are related to them. There is sometimes in such passages a fuller and a deeper meaning than the letter seems to express or than the laws of hermeneutics indicate. Moreover, the literal sense itself frequently admits other senses, which either illustrate dogma or commend morality. It must therefore be recognized that the sacred writings are wrapt in a certain religious obscurity, and that no one can enter into them without a guide. God has so disposed it that, as the Holy Fathers teach, men may investigate the Scriptures with greater ardor and earnestness, and that what is attained with difficulty may sink more deeply into the mind and heart. From this also, and mainly, men may understand that God has delivered the Scriptures to the Church, and that in reading and treating of His utterances they must follow the Church as their guide and teacher. St. Irenæus long since laid it down that where the *Charismata* of God were placed, there the truth was to be learnt, and that Scripture is expounded without peril by those with whom there is apostolic succession. His teaching, and that of other Fathers, is embraced by the Council of the Vatican which, in renewing the decree of Trent, declares its mind to be this—that "in matters of faith and morals, which belong to the building up of Christian doctrine, that sense is to be considered the true sense of the Sacred Scripture which has been held and is held by our Holy Mother the Church, whose place it is to judge of the true sense and interpretation of the Scriptures; and therefore that it is permitted to no one to interpret the Sacred Scripture contrary to this sense, or contrary to the unanimous consent of the Fathers.". By this law, most full of wisdom, the Church by no means prevents or restrains the pursuit of biblical science. She, on the contrary, provides for its freedom from error, and greatly advances its real progress. A wide field lies open to any teacher, in which his hermeneutical skill may exercise itself with signal effect and for the welfare of the Church. On the one hand, in those passages of Scripture which have not as yet received a certain and definitive interpretation, such labors may, in the sweetly ordered providence of God, serve as a preparation for bringing to maturity the judgment of the Church. In passages already defined, a private doctor may do work equally valuable, either by setting them forth more clearly to the commonalty of the faithful, or more learnedly before the learned, or by defending them more powerfully from adversaries. Wherefore the first and most sacred object of the Catholic commentator should be to interpret those passages which have received an authentic interpretation—either from the sacred writers themselves, under the inspiration of the Holy Ghost (as in many places of the New Testament), or from the Church, under the assistance of the same Holy Spirit, whether by her solemn judgment or by her ordinary and universal authoritative teaching—in that identical sense, and to prove, by all the resources of learning, that sound hermeneutical laws admit of no other than that interpretation. In the other passages the analogy of faith should be followed, and the Catholic doctrine, as authoritatively proposed by the Church, should be held as the supreme rule. Since the same God is the author both of the Sacred Books and of the doctrine committed to the Church, it is clearly impossible that any teaching can by legitimate interpretation be extracted from the former which shall in any respect be at variance with the latter. Hence it follows that all interpretation is unfounded and false which either makes the sacred writers disagree one with another, or is opposed to the doctrine of the Church.

The professor of Holy Scripture, therefore, amongst other recommendations, must be well versed in the whole of Theology, and deeply read in the commentaries of the Holy Fathers and Doctors, and the best of other interpreters. This is inculcated by St. Jerome, and still more by St. Augustine, who thus justly complains: "If there is no branch of teaching, however humble and easy to learn, which does not require a master, what can be a greater sign of rashness and pride than to refuse to study the Books of the divine mysteries by the help of those who have interpreted them?" Other Fathers have said the same, and have confirmed it by their example. They endeavored to acquire understanding of the Holy Scriptures, not by their own lights and ideas, but from the writings and authority of the ancients, who in their turn, as we know, received the rule of interpretation in direct line from the Apostles.

The Holy Fathers, to whom, after the Apostles, the Church owes its growth—who planted, watered, built, fed, and nourished it—are of supreme authority whenever they all interpret in one and the same manner any text of the Bible as pertaining to doctrine of faith or morals. Their unanimity clearly evinces that such interpretation has come down from the Apostles as a matter of Catholic faith. The opinion of the Fathers is also of very great weight when they treat of these matters in their capacity of private teachers; not only because they excelled in knowledge of revealed doctrine and in acquaintance with many things useful for the understanding of the apostolic Books, but also because they were men of eminent sanctity and of ardent zeal for the truth, on whom God bestowed a more ample measure of His light. The commentator, therefore, should make it his care to follow in their footsteps with reverence, and to avail himself of their labors with intelligent appreciation.

He must not, however, on that account consider that it is forbidden, when just cause exists, to push inquiry and exposition beyond what the Fathers have done—provided he religiously observes the rule so wisely laid down by St. Augustine: not to depart from the literal and obvious sense, except where reason makes that sense untenable or necessity requires. This is a rule to which it is the more necessary to adhere strictly in these times, when the thirst for novelty and unrestrained license of thought make the danger of error most real and proximate. Neither should those passages be neglected which the Fathers have understood in an allegorical or figurative sense, more especially when such interpretation is justified by the literal sense, and when it rests on the authority of many. This method of interpretation has been received by the Church from the Apostles, and has been approved by her own practice, as her liturgy attests. The Holy Fathers did not thereby pretend directly to demonstrate dogmas of faith, but used it as a means of promoting virtue and piety, such as, by their own experience, they knew to be most valuable.

The authority of other Catholic interpreters is not so grave. Since, however, the study of Scripture has always continued to advance in the Church, their commentaries also have their own honorable place, and are serviceable in many ways for the refutation of assailants and the unravelling of difficulties. It is, moreover, most unbecoming to pass by, in ignorance or contempt, the splendid works which our own scholars have left behind them in abundance, and to have recourse to the works of the heterodox, and to seek in them, with peril to sound doctrine and not seldom with detriment to faith, the explanation of passages on which Catholics have long ago most excellently expended their talents and their labor. Although the studies of the heterodox, used with prudence, may sometimes be of use to the Catholic interpreter, he should nevertheless bear well in mind this repeated testimony of the ancients,—that the sense of the Sacred Scriptures can nowhere be found incorrupt outside the Church, and that it cannot be delivered by those who, being destitute of the true faith, only gnaw the husk of Scripture and never reach its marrow.

Most desirable it is, and most essential, that the whole course of Theology should be pervaded by the use of the Divine Scripture, which should be, as it were, the soul thereof. This is what the Fathers and the greatest

theologians of all ages have professed and practised. It
was chiefly out of the sacred writings that they endeavored to proclaim and establish the Articles of Faith and
the truths which are their consequences. It was in
them, together with divine tradition, that they found
the refutation of heretical error, and the reasonableness,
the true meaning, and the mutual relation of the truths
of the Catholic faith. Nor will any one wonder at this
who considers that the Sacred Books hold such a pre-
eminent position among the sources of Revelation that
without the assiduous study of them Theology cannot
be rightly treated as its dignity demands. Although it
is right and proper that students in academical institutions and schools should be chiefly exercised in acquir-
ing a scientific knowledge of dogma by means of reasoning from the Articles of Faith to their consequences,
according to the rules of approved and solid philosophy,
nevertheless a grave and learned theologian will by
no means overlook that method of doctrinal demonstra-
tion which draws its proof from the authority of the
Bible. Theology does not receive her first principles
from other sciences, but immediately from God through
Revelation. And therefore she does not receive from
other sciences as from superiors, but uses them as her
inferiors and her handmaids. It is this view of doctrinal
teaching which is laid down and recommended by the
prince of theologians, St. Thomas of Aquin. He also
shows—such being the essential character of Christian
Theology—how a theologian can defend his own principles against attack. "If the adversary," he says, "do
but grant any portion of the divine revelation, we have
an argument against him. Against a heretic we can
employ Scripture authority, and against those who deny
one article we can use another. If our opponent rejects
divine revelation altogether, then there is no way left
to prove the Articles of Faith by reasoning. We can
only solve the difficulties which are raised against the

faith." Care must be taken, then, that beginners approach the study of the Bible well prepared and furnished; otherwise, just hopes will be frustrated, or perchance—and this is worse—they will unthinkingly risk the danger of error, and fall an easy prey to the sophisms and labored erudition of the rationalists. The best preparation will be a conscientious application to philosophy and theology under the guidance of St. Thomas of Aquin, and a thorough training therein—as We Ourselves have elsewhere shown and prescribed. By this means, both in biblical studies and in that part of Theology which is called *Positive*, they will pursue the right path and make solid progress.

To prove, to expound, to illustrate Catholic doctrine by the legitimate and skilful interpretation of the Bible is much; but there is a second part of the subject of equal importance and of equal laboriousness,—the maintenance in the strongest possible way of the fulness of its authority. This cannot be done completely or satisfactorily except by means of the living teaching authority of the Church herself. The Church, by reason of her wonderful propagation, her shining sanctity, and her inexhaustible fecundity in good, her Catholic unity, and her unshaken stability, is herself a great and perpetual motive of credibility, and an unassailable testimony of her own divine mission. But since the divine and infallible teaching authority of the Church rests also on the authority of Holy Scripture, the first thing to be done is to vindicate the trustworthiness of the sacred records at least as human documents. From this can clearly be proved, as from primitive and authentic testimony, the divinity and the mission of Christ our Lord, the institution of a hierarchical Church, and the primacy of Peter and his successors. It is most desirable, therefore, that there should be many members of the clergy well prepared to enter upon a contest of this nature, and to repulse the attacks of the enemy, chiefly trusting in that armor of God which is recommended by the Apostle, but at the same time not unacquainted with the more modern methods of attack. This is beautifully alluded to by St. John Chrysostom. Describing the duties of priests, he says: "We must use our every endeavor that the 'word of God may dwell in us abundantly.' Not merely for one kind of fight must we be prepared, for the contest is many-sided, and the enemy is of every sort. They do not all use the same weapons, nor do all make their onset in the same way. It is needful that the man who has to contend against all should have knowledge of the engines and the arts of all. He must be at once archer and slinger, commandant and officer, general and private soldier, foot-soldier and horseman, skilled in sea-fight and in siege. Unless he knows every trick and turn of war, the devil is well able, if only a single door be left open, to get in his ferocious bandits and to carry off the sheep." The sophisms of the enemy and the manifold strategy of his attack We have already touched upon.

Let Us now say a word of advice on the means of defence. The first means is the study of Oriental languages and of the art of criticism. These two acquirements are in these days held in high estimation. The clergy, by making themselves more or less fully acquainted with them, as time and place may demand, will the better be able to discharge their office with becoming credit. They must make themselves "all things to all men," always "ready to satisfy every one that asketh them a reason for the hope that is in them." Hence it is most proper that professors of Sacred Scripture and theologians should master those tongues in which the Sacred Books were originally written. It would be well that Church students also should cultivate them, more especially those who aspire to academic degrees in Theology. Endeavors should be made to establish in all academic institutions—as has already been laudably done in many—chairs of the other ancient languages, especially the Semitic, and of subjects connected therewith, for the benefit principally of those who are destined to profess sacred literature. These latter, with a similar object in view, should make themselves well acquainted with and thoroughly exercised in the art of true criticism. There has arisen, to the great damage of religion, an artificial method, which is dignified by the name of the "higher criticism." It pretends to judge of the origin, the integrity, and the authority of every Book from internal indications alone. It is clear, on the other hand, that in historical questions, such as the origin and the handing down of writings, the witness of history is of primary importance, and that historical investigation should be made with the utmost care. In this matter internal evidence is seldom of great value, except by way of confirmation. To look upon it in any other light will be to open the door to many evil consequences. It will make the enemies of religion much more bold and confident in attacking and endeavoring to destroy the authenticity of the Sacred Books. This vaunted "higher criticism" will resolve itself into the reflection of the bias and the prejudice of the critics. It will not throw on the Scriptures the light which is sought, or prove of any advantage to doctrine. It will only give rise to disagreement and dissension, those sure notes of error, which the critics in question so plentifully exhibit in their own persons. Seeing that most of them are tainted with false philosophy and rationalism, it must lead to the elimination from the sacred writings of all prophecy and all miracle, and of everything else that lies outside the natural order.

In the second place, we have to contend against those who, abusing their knowledge of physical science, minutely scrutinize the Sacred Books, in order to detect the writers in a mistake, and so to vilify the books themselves. Attacks of this kind, bearing as they do on matters of experience of the senses, are peculiarly dangerous to the masses, and also to the young, who are but beginning their literary studies. The young, if they lose their reverence for divine revelation on any one point, are but too easily led to give up believing in revelation altogether. It need scarcely be pointed out how the science of nature, just as it is so admirably adapted to show forth the glory of the Great Creator, provided it be rightly taught, so, if it be perversely imparted to the youthful intelligence, it may prove most fatal in destroying the principles of true philosophy, and in the corruption of morality. Hence to the professor of Sacred Scripture a knowledge of natural science will be of the greatest service in detecting and meeting such attacks upon the Sacred Books.

There can never, indeed, be any real discrepancy between the theologian and the physicist, as long as each confines himself within his own lines, and so long as both are careful, as St. Augustine warns us, "not to make rash assertions, or to assert that which is not known as if it were really known." If dissension should arise between them, here is the rule, laid down by St. Augustine for the theologian: "Whatever they can really demonstrate to be true of physical nature, we must show to be not contrary to our Scriptures. Whatever they assert in their treatises which is contrary to these Scriptures of ours, that is, to Catholic faith, we must either prove it, as well as we can, to be entirely false, or at all events we must, without the smallest hesitation, believe it to be so." To understand how just is the rule here formulated we must remember, first, that the sacred writers, or, to speak more accurately, the Holy Ghost, who spoke by means of them, did not intend to teach men those things (that is to say, the essential nature of the things of the visible universe)—things which are in no way profitable unto salvation. The sacred writers did not seek to penetrate the secrets of nature. They rather described and dealt with things in more or less figurative language, or in terms which were commonly used at the time, and terms which in many instances are in daily use at this day, even amongst the most eminent men of science. Ordinary speech primarily and properly describes that which falls under the senses. Somewhat in the same way the sacred writers—as the Angelic Doctor reminds us—" went by what sensibly appeared," or put down that which God, speaking to men, signified in a way which men could understand, and to which they were accustomed.

The strenuous defence of the Holy Scripture, however, does not require that we should equally uphold all the opinions which every one of the Fathers, or which subsequent commentators have set forth in explaining it. It may be that, in commenting on passages where physical matters are in question, they have sometimes expressed the ideas of their own times, and have thus made statements which in these days have been abandoned as unfounded. In their interpretations, therefore, we must carefully note that which they lay down as belonging to faith, or as intimately connected with faith, or that in which they are unanimous. "In those things which do not come under the obligation of faith, the Saints were at liberty to hold divergent opinions, even as we ourselves are," says St. Thomas. In another place he says most admirably: "When philosophers are agreed upon a point, and that point is not contrary to faith, it is safer, in my opinion, neither to lay down such a point as a dogma of faith, even though it is perhaps so presented by the philosophers, nor to reject it as against faith, lest we thus give to the wise of this world an occasion of despising the doctrine of the faith." The Catholic commentator, although he should show that those facts of natural science which investigators affirm to be now in these days absolutely certain are not contrary to Scripture rightly explained, must nevertheless always bear in mind that much which has been held as

proved and certain has afterwards been called in question
and rejected. If writers on physics travel outside the
boundaries of their own department, and carry their er-
roneous teaching into the domain of philosophy, let
them be handed over by the theological commentator to
philosophers for refutation.

The principles here laid down will apply to cognate
sciences, and especially to history. It is a lamentable
fact that there are many men who with great labor make
and publish investigations on the monuments of antiquity,
the manners and institutions of nations, and other illus-
trative subjects, and whose chief purpose in all this is
too often to try to find mistakes in the sacred writings,
and so to shake and weaken their authority. Some of
these writers display not only extreme hostility, but also
great unfairness. In their eyes a profane book or an
ancient document is accepted without hesitation. Scripture, if they can only find in it a suspicion of error, is
set down with the slightest possible discussion as being
entirely untrustworthy. It is true, no doubt, that copyists have made mistakes in the text of the Bible. This
question, when it arises, should be carefully considered
on its merits. The fact, however, is not to be too easily
admitted, but only in those passages where the proof is
clear. It may also happen that the sense of a passage
remains ambiguous. In this case, sound hermeneutical
methods will greatly aid in clearing up obscurity. It is
absolutely wrong, however, and it is forbidden, either
to narrow inspiration to certain parts only of Holy Scripture, or to admit that the sacred writer has erred. The
system of those who, in order to rid themselves of these
difficulties, do not hesitate to concede that divine inspiration regards matters of faith and morals, and nothing beyond them, because (as they wrongly think) in a
question of the truth or falsehood of a passage we should
consider not so much what God has said as the reason
and purpose which He had in mind in saying it, cannot

be tolerated. All the books which the Church receives as sacred and canonical were written wholly and entirely, with all their parts, at the dictation of the Holy Ghost. So far is it from being possible that any error can co-exist with inspiration, inspiration not only is essentially incompatible with error, but it excludes error as absolutely and necessarily as it is impossible that God Himself, the Supreme Truth, can utter that which is not true. This is the ancient and unchanging faith of the Church. It was solemnly defined in the Councils of Florence and of Trent. It was finally confirmed and more expressly formulated by the Council of the Vatican. These are the words of that Council: The Books of the Old and of the New Testament, whole and entire, with all their parts, as they are enumerated in the decree of the same Council (Trent), and as they are contained in the old Latin Vulgate edition, are to be received as sacred and canonical. The Church holds them as sacred and canonical, not because, having been composed solely by human industry, they were afterwards approved by her authority, nor only because they contain revelation without error, but because, having been written under the inspiration of the Holy Ghost, they have God for their Author. Hence we cannot say that, because the Holy Ghost employed men as His instruments, it was these inspired instruments who, perchance, have fallen into error, and not the primary Author. By supernatural power He so moved and impelled them to write—He was so present to them—that all the things which He ordered, and those things only, they first rightly conceived, then willed faithfully to write down, and finally expressed in adequate words and with infallible truth. Otherwise, it could not be said that He was the Author of the whole of the Sacred Scripture. Such has always been the persuasion of the Fathers. "Therefore," says St. Augustine, "since they wrote the things which He showed and said to them, it cannot be said that He did not write them. His members executed that which their Head dictated." St. Gregory the Great maintains: "Most superfluous it is to inquire who wrote these things;—we loyally believe the Holy Ghost to be the Author of the Book. He wrote it who dictated it to be written. He wrote it who inspired its execution."

It follows that those men who maintain that an error is possible in any genuine passage of the sacred writings, either pervert the Catholic notion of inspiration, or make God Himself to be the Author of error. So emphatically were all the Fathers and Doctors agreed that the divine writings, as left by the hagiographers, are entirely free from all error, that they labored earnestly, with no less skill than reverence, to reconcile one with the other those numerous passages which seem to be at variance—the very passages which in great measure have been taken up by the "higher criticism." The Fathers were unanimous in laying it down that those writings, in their entirety and in all their parts, were equally from the divine *afflatus*, and that God Himself, speaking through the sacred writers, could not set down anything that was not true. The words of St. Augustine to St. Jerome may sum up what they taught: "On my own part, I confess to your charity that it is only to those Books of Scripture which are now called canonical that I have learned to pay such honor and reverence as to believe most firmly that no one of their writers has fallen into any error. If in these Books I meet with anything which seems contrary to truth, I shall not hesitate to conclude either that the text is faulty, or that the translator has not expressed the meaning of the passage, or that I myself have not understood it."

But with all the weapons of the best of arts, fully and perfectly to fight for the holiness of the Bible is far more than can be looked for from the exertions of commentators and theologians alone. It is an enterprise in which we have a right to expect the co-operation of all Catholic men who have acquired reputation in other branches of learning. As in the past, so at the present time the Church is never without the graceful support of her accomplished children. May their services to the Faith ever grow and increase! There is nothing which We believe to be more needful than that truth should find defenders more powerful and more numerous than are the enemies whom it has to face. There is nothing which is better calculated to imbue the masses with homage for the truth than to see it joyously proclaimed by learned men who have gained distinction in some other faculty. Moreover, the bitter tongues of objectors will be silenced. At least they will not dare to insist so shamelessly that faith is the enemy of science when they see that scientific men, of eminence in their own profession, show towards the faith most marked honor and reverence.

Seeing, then, that those men can do so much for the progress of religion on whom the goodness of God has bestowed, together with the grace of the faith, great natural talent, let such men, in this most savage conflict of which the Scriptures are now the object, select each of them the branch of study which is best adapted to his circumstances, and endeavor to excel therein, and thus be prepared to repel with effect and credit the assaults on the word of God. It is our pleasing duty to give deserved praise to a work which certain Catholics have taken in hand—that is to say, the formation of societies, and the contribution of considerable sums of money, for the purpose of aiding certain of the more learned in the pursuit of their study to its completeness. Truly, an excellent method of investing money! It is an investment most suited to the times in which we live! The less hope of public patronage there is for Catholic study, the more ready and the more abundant should be the liberality of private persons. Those to whom God has given riches will thus use them to safeguard the treasure of His revealed doctrine.

In order that such labors may prove of real service to the cause of the Bible, let scholars keep steadfastly to the principles which we have in this Letter laid down. Let them loyally hold that God, the Creator and the Ruler of all things, is also the Author of the Scriptures —and that therefore nothing can possibly be proved, either by physical science or by archeology, which can be in real contradiction with the Scriptures. If apparent contradictions should be met with, every effort should be made to meet them. Theologians and commentators of solid judgment should be consulted as to what is the true or the most probable meaning of the passage in discussion. Adverse arguments should also be carefully weighed. Even if the difficulty is not after all cleared up, and the discrepancy seems to remain, the contest must not be abandoned. Truth cannot contradict truth. We may be sure that some mistake has been made, either in the interpretation of the sacred words, or in the polemical discussion itself. If no mistake can be detected, we must then suspend judgment for the time being. There have been objections without number perseveringly directed against the Scriptures for many a long year. These have been proved to be futile, and they are now never heard of. Interpretations not a few have been put on certain passages of Scripture (not belonging to the rule of faith or morals), and these have been rectified after a more careful investigation. As time goes on mistaken views die and disappear. Truth remaineth and groweth stronger for ever and ever. Wherefore, as no one should be so presumptuous as to think that he understands the whole of the Scriptures—in which St. Augustine himself confessed that there was more that he did not know than that which he did know—so, if one should come upon anything that seems incapable of solution, he must take to heart the cautious rule of the same holy Doctor: "It is better even to be oppressed by unknown but useful signs than to interpret them uselessly, and thus to throw off the yoke of servitude only to be caught in the nets of error."

As regards those men who pursue the subsidiary studies of which We have spoken, if they honestly and modestly follow the counsels and commands which We have given—if by pen and voice they make their studies fruitful against the enemies of the truth, and useful in saving the young from loss of faith—they may justly congratulate themselves on worthy service to the Sacred Writings, and on their having afforded to the Catholic religion that aid which the Church has a right to expect from the piety and from the learning of her children.

Such, Venerable Brethren, are the admonitions and the instructions which, by the help of God, We have thought it well, at the present moment, to offer to you on the study of the Sacred Scriptures. It will now be for you to see that what We have said be held and observed with all due reverence, that so we may prove our gratitude to God for the communication to man of the words of His wisdom, and that all the good results which are so much to be desired may be realized, especially as they effect the training of the students of the Church, which is matter of Our own great solicitude and of the Church's hope. Exert yourselves with glad alacrity, and use your authority, and your persuasive powers, in order that these studies may be held in just regard, and that they may flourish in the seminaries and in the educational institutions which are under your jurisdiction. May they flourish in the completeness of success, under the direction of the Church, in accordance with the salutary teaching and the example of the Holy Fathers, and the laudable traditions of antiquity. As time goes on, let them be widened and extended as the interests and glory of the truth may require—the interests of that Catholic Truth which comes down from above, the never-failing source of the salvation of all peoples. Finally,

We admonish with paternal love all students and ministers of the Church always to approach the sacred writings with the most profound affection of reverence and of piety. It is impossible to attain to a profitable understanding thereof unless, laying aside the arrogance of "earthly" science, there be excited in the heart a holy desire for that wisdom " which is from above." In this way the mind which has once entered on these sacred studies, and which has by means of them been enlightened and strengthened, will acquire a marvellous facility in detecting and avoiding the fallacies of human science, and in gathering and utilizing solid fruit for eternal salvation. The heart will then wax warm, and will strive with more ardent longing to advance in virtue and in divine love. "Blessed are they who examine His testimonies; they shall seek Him with their whole heart."

And now, filled with hope in the divine assistance, and trusting to your pastoral solicitude—as a pledge of heavenly graces and in witness of Our special good will —to all of you, and to the clergy, and to the whole flock which has been intrusted to you, We most lovingly impart in our Lord the Apostolic Benediction.

Given at St. Peter's, at Rome, the 18th day of November, 1893, the sixteenth year of Our Pontificate.

LEO PP. XIII.

www.ingramcontent.com/pod-product-compliance
Lightning Source LLC
Chambersburg PA
CBHW020247170426
43202CB00008B/261